AMSTERDAM & THE NETHERLANDS

The Ultimate Travel Companion for an Unforgettable Dutch Adventure

MARSAI JACKSON

Copyright © 2025 by Marsai Jackson

All rights reserved. No part of this publication may be reproduced, distributed, or transmitted in any form or by any means, including photocopying, recording, or other electronic or mechanical methods, without the prior written permission of the publisher, except in the case of brief quotations embodied in critical reviews and certain other non-commercial uses permitted by copyright law.

TABLE OF CONTENTS

INTRODUCTION..................................7
CHAPTER 1 15
PLANNING YOUR DUTCH ESCAPE........ 15
   The Best Time to Visit the Netherlands
   15
   How to Get to the Netherlands......... 21
   Visa and Entry Requirements........... 25
   Travel Insurance Essentials 28
CHAPTER 2 33
GETTING AROUND THE NETHERLANDS 33
   Public Transportation: An Efficient
   Network... 33
   Local Transportation Apps: Your Digital
   Travel Assistants 43
   Bike Rentals and Cycling Routes: Pedal
   Your Way Through Paradise 47
   Car Rentals: Freedom to Explore at
   Your Own Pace............................... 54
   Local Transportation Options 62
CHAPTER 3 65

MONEY MATTERS AND PRACTICALITIES 65
   Currency Exchange Locations and Tips 65
   Money Matters: Budgeting and Costs 70
   Electricity and Plug Adapters 79
   Internet and Communication 82
CHAPTER 4 89
AMSTERDAM - THE ICONIC CAPITAL ... 89
   Must-See Areas in Amsterdam 89
   Historical Landmarks and Monuments in Amsterdam 97
   Museums in Amsterdam: A Cultural Feast 104
   Free Tourist Attractions in Amsterdam 112
   Paid Tourist Attractions in Amsterdam 116
   Off the Beaten Paths and Hidden Gems in Amsterdam 122
   Fun Places and Parks in Amsterdam 127
CHAPTER 5 131
BEYOND AMSTERDAM - EXPLORING THE NETHERLANDS 131

    Must-See Areas Outside Amsterdam 131

    Day Trips and Excursions from Amsterdam 144

    Historical Landmarks and Monuments Beyond Amsterdam 150

    Museums Beyond Amsterdam: Regional Culture and History 159

    Off the Beaten Paths and Hidden Gems Beyond Amsterdam 166

CHAPTER 6 175

LOCAL CUISINE AND DINING 175

    Local Cuisine and Must-Try Dishes .. 175

    Dining for Different Travelers 185

    Street Food Guide: A Culinary Adventure on the Go 191

CHAPTER 7 196

CULTURE, AND ENTERTAINMENT 196

    Local Festivals and Celebrations Throughout the Year 196

    Nightlife and Entertainment 206

CHAPTER 8 212

SHOPPING IN THE NETHERLANDS 212

Shopping Guide: What to Buy and Where 212

Shopping Districts and Malls 223

Local Souvenir Guide: Unique Dutch Keepsakes.................................. 231

CHAPTER 9 237

NATURE AND OUTDOOR ADVENTURES 237

Local Boat Tours and Cruises 237

CHAPTER 10 245

ACCOMMODATIONS IN THE NETHERLANDS 245

Accommodation Guide by Traveler Type 245

Accommodation by Price Range 254

Accommodation by Location 258

CHAPTER 11 263

PRACTICAL TIPS AND RESOURCES ... 263

Travel Scams and How to Avoid Them 263

INTRODUCTION

A Land of Canals, Windmills, and Golden Age History

Imagine a place where elegant canals crisscross charming cities, historic windmills dot the green countryside, and a rich history comes alive at every turn. This is the Netherlands! For centuries, canals have been the lifeblood of Dutch cities, not just for transportation but also shaping the landscape and culture. Think of the iconic canals of Amsterdam, a UNESCO World Heritage site, where you can glide along on a boat tour, passing by beautiful canal houses.

Windmills are another quintessential Dutch symbol. Originally built for practical purposes like draining water and grinding grain, they are now cherished landmarks.

You can visit places like Zaanse Schans or Kinderdijk to see well-preserved windmills and learn about their history. Kinderdijk, with its network of nineteen windmills, is also a UNESCO site and offers a fantastic glimpse into Dutch water management ingenuity.

And then there's the Golden Age, a period in the 17th century when the Dutch Republic was a global powerhouse in trade, science, military, and art. This era left an indelible mark on the Netherlands, evident in its stunning art (think Rembrandt and Vermeer), grand architecture, and museums filled with treasures from around the world. Visiting museums like the Rijksmuseum in Amsterdam will transport you back to this fascinating period.

Why Choose the Netherlands for Your Next Trip?

Why indeed? The Netherlands offers a unique blend of experiences that appeal to a wide range of travelers. Are you interested in culture and history? The Netherlands boasts world-class museums, historic cities, and a captivating past. Love art? You're in the land of Van Gogh, Rembrandt, and Vermeer! Prefer nature? Explore the tulip fields in spring, cycle through scenic countryside, or relax on the beaches of the North Sea coast.

Beyond the iconic sights, the Netherlands is incredibly easy to navigate, with excellent public transportation and English widely spoken. It's a safe and welcoming country, perfect for solo travelers, families, couples, and everyone in between. Whether you're seeking a romantic honeymoon, a fun family vacation, or a solo exploration, the Netherlands has something special to offer. Plus, its compact size means you can experience a lot in a relatively short trip!

And let's not forget the "gezelligheid" - a Dutch concept that embodies coziness, conviviality, and a general sense of well-being. You'll find it in the charming cafes, friendly locals, and relaxed atmosphere that permeates Dutch life.

Brief Overview of Amsterdam and Key Regions

While Amsterdam is often the first city that comes to mind, the Netherlands is more than just its capital. Let's take a quick tour of some key regions:

- **Amsterdam:** The vibrant heart of the Netherlands, famous for its canals, museums (like the Anne Frank House, Rijksmuseum, Van Gogh Museum), and lively atmosphere. It's a city for walking, cycling, and soaking in the unique urban vibe.

- **The Hague (Den Haag):** The political center of the Netherlands and home to international organizations like the International Court of Justice. It's a sophisticated city with royal palaces, grand boulevards, and the beach resort of Scheveningen nearby.

- **Rotterdam:** A city of modern architecture, rebuilt after WWII. Rotterdam is known for its innovative buildings, bustling port, and vibrant cultural scene. It's a stark contrast to Amsterdam's historic charm, offering a different, equally compelling Dutch experience.

- **Utrecht:** Located in the heart of the Netherlands, Utrecht boasts a beautiful medieval city center with unique wharf cellars along its canals. The Dom Tower, the tallest church tower in the Netherlands, dominates the skyline. It's a charming city with a relaxed pace.

- **The Dutch Countryside:** Beyond the cities, you'll find picturesque landscapes of tulip fields (especially in spring), windmills, charming villages like Giethoorn, and coastal areas. Exploring the countryside by bike is a classic Dutch experience.

Setting Expectations: What Makes the Netherlands Unique

To truly appreciate the Netherlands, it's helpful to understand some of its unique characteristics. Firstly, **it's flat!** This makes it ideal for cycling, but also means you won't find dramatic mountains. Secondly, **the weather can be unpredictable.** Be prepared for rain and wind, even in summer. Packing layers and waterproof gear is always a good idea.

The Dutch are direct and efficient. Customer service might be less overly solicitous than in some other countries, but it's generally efficient and helpful. **English is widely spoken**, especially in tourist areas, but learning a few basic Dutch phrases is always appreciated. **Cycling is a way of life.** Be mindful of bike lanes and cyclists, and consider joining the locals on two wheels! Finally, **be prepared for crowds, especially in Amsterdam**, particularly during peak season. Booking accommodations and popular attractions in advance is highly recommended.

CHAPTER 1

PLANNING YOUR DUTCH ESCAPE

The Best Time to Visit the Netherlands

Choosing the right time to visit can significantly impact your experience. The Netherlands has distinct seasons, each offering its own charm and activities.

- **Seasonal Guide: Spring Blooms, Summer Festivals, Autumn Colors, Winter Charm**
    - **Spring (March - May):** Spring is synonymous with tulips in the Netherlands! Keukenhof Gardens is a must-visit, bursting with millions of blooming flowers. King's Day

(April 27th) is a massive national celebration with street parties and orange everywhere. The weather starts to warm up, making it pleasant for cycling and outdoor activities.

- **Summer (June - August):** Summer is festival season! Enjoy outdoor music festivals, canal festivals, and beach days. The weather is generally warm and sunny, perfect for exploring cities and enjoying the outdoors. However, it's also peak tourist season, so expect higher prices and more crowds.

- **Autumn (September - October):** Autumn brings

beautiful fall foliage, especially in parks and forests. The crowds thin out, and prices may be lower. It's a great time for cycling through colorful landscapes and enjoying cozy cafes. The weather can be crisp and cool, with occasional rain.

- **Winter (November - February):** Winter in the Netherlands is charming in its own way. Amsterdam Light Festival illuminates the canals in December and January. If it's cold enough, canals might freeze over for ice skating – a truly unique Dutch experience! Christmas markets add festive cheer. Be prepared for cold, damp weather and shorter daylight hours.

- **Weather Patterns and Considerations for Each Season**
    - **Spring:** Temperatures range from cool to mild (averaging 8-15°C or 46-59°F). Expect some rain, especially in early spring. Pack layers and a light waterproof jacket.
    - **Summer:** Warm and pleasant, with average temperatures around 17-20°C (63-68°F), but can reach higher. Sunshine is more frequent, but rain is still possible. Pack light clothing, but have layers for cooler evenings.

- **Autumn:** Temperatures cool down (averaging 10-15°C or 50-59°F). Increased chance of rain and wind. Pack layers, waterproof outerwear, and comfortable walking shoes.
- **Winter:** Cold and damp, with average temperatures around 0-5°C (32-41°F). Chance of snow and ice. Pack warm layers, waterproof and windproof outerwear, hat, gloves, and scarf.

- **Peak and Off-Peak Travel Times: Pros and Cons**
    - **Peak Season (Spring & Summer):**
        - **Pros:** Best weather, tulip season, festivals,

long daylight hours, vibrant atmosphere.

- **Cons:** Higher prices for flights and accommodation, larger crowds at attractions, need to book well in advance.

- **Off-Peak Season (Autumn & Winter):**
  - **Pros:** Lower prices, fewer crowds, unique seasonal experiences (autumn colors, winter markets, ice skating), cozy atmosphere.
  - **Cons:** Colder and wetter weather, shorter daylight hours, some attractions may have

reduced hours or be closed.

How to Get to the Netherlands

The Netherlands is well-connected to the rest of the world, making it easily accessible by air, train, ferry, and bus.

- **Flying into Amsterdam Schiphol Airport (AMS) and Other International Airports**

Amsterdam Schiphol Airport (AMS) is the main international airport and one of the busiest in Europe. It offers direct flights from countless cities worldwide. It's located just outside Amsterdam and has excellent train connections to the city center (approx. 15-20 minutes). You can easily find train tickets directly at the airport Schiphol Plaza.

Other international airports include:

- **Rotterdam The Hague Airport (RTM):** Serves Rotterdam and The Hague. Good for reaching these cities directly and also well-connected to Amsterdam by train (though with a change).

- **Eindhoven Airport (EIN):** Located in the south, primarily served by budget airlines. Useful for reaching Eindhoven and the southern Netherlands. Train connections are available to Eindhoven city center and beyond.

- **Train Travel from Neighboring European Countries**

The Netherlands is part of Europe's extensive high-speed rail network. High-speed trains like Thalys (from Paris and Brussels), ICE (from Germany), and Eurostar (indirectly via Brussels) connect the Netherlands to major European cities. Amsterdam Centraal Station is the main international train hub. Booking train tickets in advance, especially for high-speed trains, is recommended for better prices. Websites like (https://www.nsinternational.com/en) are great resources for booking and information.

- **Ferry and Bus Options**
    - **Ferries:** Ferries connect the Netherlands to the UK (e.g., Newcastle to Amsterdam with

https://www.dfds.com/en), and other countries across the North Sea. Ferry travel can be a scenic and relaxing way to arrive, especially if you're bringing a car.

- **Buses:** International bus companies like FlixBus and Eurolines offer budget-friendly travel to the Netherlands from various European cities. Bus travel is generally slower than trains but can be a more economical option. Bus stations are typically located in or near city centers.

Visa and Entry Requirements

Understanding visa requirements is crucial for a hassle-free trip.

- **Schengen Area Information and Visa Regulations**

The Netherlands is part of the Schengen Area, a zone of 29 European countries that have abolished passport and border control at their common borders. For many nationalities, including those from the USA, Canada, Australia, and the UK, you can enter the Schengen Area for tourism or business for up to 90 days within a 180-day period without a visa. However, always **check the specific visa requirements based on your nationality** well in advance of your trip. The official website of the Netherlands Immigration and Naturalisation Service

(IND) is the best resource for up-to-date information.

- **Passport and Documentation Checklist**

Regardless of visa requirements, ensure you have the following:

- **Valid Passport:** Your passport must be valid for at least three months beyond your intended stay in the Schengen Area. It's always safer to have at least six months of validity remaining.

- **Return or Onward Ticket:** You may be asked to show proof of onward travel (e.g., a return flight ticket) when entering the Schengen Area.

- **Proof of Accommodation:** Have your hotel or accommodation booking details readily available.

- **Proof of Sufficient Funds:** Be prepared to demonstrate that you have enough money to support yourself during your stay. This could be bank statements or credit card information.

- **Travel Insurance (Recommended):** While not always mandatory for short stays, travel insurance is highly recommended for peace of mind (more on this below).

- **Driving License (if applicable):** If you plan to

rent a car, bring your valid driving license and consider an International Driving Permit.

Travel Insurance Essentials

Travel insurance is an essential part of responsible travel planning.

- **Why Travel Insurance is Crucial**

Unexpected events can happen, and travel insurance provides a safety net. It can cover:

- **Medical Emergencies:** Medical care in foreign countries can be expensive. Insurance can cover medical bills, hospitalization, and emergency evacuation if needed.

- **Trip Cancellation or Interruption:** If you have to cancel your trip due to illness, family emergencies, or other unforeseen circumstances, insurance can reimburse non-refundable costs. Trip interruption coverage can help if your trip is cut short.

- **Lost or Delayed Baggage:** Insurance can compensate you for lost, stolen, or delayed luggage, helping with essential replacements.

- **Personal Liability:** Coverage if you accidentally cause damage or injury to someone else.

- **Theft or Loss of Personal Belongings:** Protection

against theft of your belongings.

- **Types of Coverage to Consider**

    - **Medical Insurance:** Essential for covering medical expenses abroad. Check the coverage limits and ensure it includes emergency medical evacuation.

    - **Trip Cancellation and Interruption Insurance:** Covers financial losses if your trip is cancelled or interrupted for covered reasons.

    - **Baggage Insurance:** Protects against lost, delayed, or damaged luggage.

    - **Activity-Specific Insurance:** If you plan to

engage in adventure sports or specific high-risk activities, ensure your policy covers these.

- **Choosing the Right Policy for Your Trip**

    - **Assess Your Needs:** Consider your age, health, pre-existing conditions, planned activities, and the value of your trip when choosing coverage.

    - **Compare Policies:** Get quotes from different insurance providers and compare coverage, exclusions, and prices. Websites like World Nomads or Allianz Travel Insurance are good places to start comparing.

- **Read the Fine Print:** Understand what is and isn't covered by the policy. Pay attention to exclusions and limitations.

- **Ensure Adequate Coverage Limits:** Choose coverage limits that are sufficient for potential medical expenses and trip costs.

- **24/7 Assistance:** Opt for a policy that offers 24/7 emergency assistance services.

CHAPTER 2

GETTING AROUND THE NETHERLANDS

Public Transportation: An Efficient Network

The Dutch public transportation system is a marvel of efficiency, making it easy to travel between cities, towns, and even within urban areas. It's a network of **trains, trams, buses, and ferries** that work seamlessly together.

- **Understanding the Dutch Public Transportation System:**
  - **Trains (Trein):** The backbone of long-distance travel. Nederlandse Spoorwegen (NS) is the main train operator. Trains are

frequent, punctual, and comfortable, connecting cities across the country. You can use trains to travel from Amsterdam to Rotterdam, The Hague, Utrecht, and beyond.

- **Trams (Tram):** Primarily found in cities like Amsterdam, Rotterdam, The Hague, and Utrecht. Trams are ideal for getting around within the city, especially in the center where streets can be narrow.

- **Buses (Bus):** Extensive bus networks operate in cities and rural areas, filling in the gaps where trains and trams don't reach. Regional bus companies complement the urban networks.

- **Ferries (Veerboot):** Essential for reaching islands (like the Wadden Islands) and crossing waterways, especially in and around Amsterdam and Rotterdam. Some ferries within cities are even free!
- **Navigating the "OV-chipkaart" (Public Transport Card):**

The **OV-chipkaart** is a rechargeable smart card used for all public transport in the Netherlands. Think of it as your all-in-one ticket to trains, trams, and buses. It's the most convenient way to pay for travel.

- **Types of OV-chipkaart:**
    - **Personal OV-chipkaart:** Linked to your name and photo, valid for 5 years, and can be used for discounted travel if you are eligible (like residents with subscriptions). Not typically for short-term visitors.
    - **Anonymous OV-chipkaart:** Reusable and can be purchased by anyone. Valid for 5 years. A good option for tourists planning to use public transport frequently over a few

days or longer trips. You can buy these at NS ticket machines at train stations, some supermarkets, and tobacco shops.

- **Disposable OV-chipkaart:** Single-use or limited-use cards, less economical for frequent travel. Best for occasional trips or if you don't want to deal with recharging.

- **How to Use the OV-chipkaart:**

    - **Check-in:** Hold your card to the card reader at the start of your journey. You'll hear a beep or see a green light. Do this when entering a train station platform, getting on a tram or bus.

- **Check-out:** Hold your card to the reader again at the end of your journey. This calculates the fare and deducts it from your card balance. Do this when leaving a train station platform, getting off a tram or bus. **Crucially, remember to always check-out, or you might be overcharged!**

- **Purchasing Tickets and Passes:**

While the OV-chipkaart is recommended, there are other ticket options:

- **Single-Use Tickets:** Available for trams and buses, usually purchased on board from the driver or conductor (often more expensive than using an OV-chipkaart).

- **Day Tickets/Multi-Day Passes:** Offered by city transportation companies (like GVB in Amsterdam, RET in Rotterdam, HTM in The Hague). These provide unlimited travel within a city for a set period (e.g., 24, 48, 72 hours). Great value for city exploration. You can buy these online through the respective transport company websites or apps, or at ticket vending machines.

- **NS Train Tickets:** For train travel, you can buy single-journey tickets or day return tickets from NS ticket machines at train stations or online via the NS website. For longer journeys, consider booking in advance for potential discounts.

- **"Holland Travel Ticket":** A day ticket offering unlimited travel on all public transport throughout the Netherlands for one calendar day. A good option for extensive day trips across the country, but more expensive than city-specific day tickets. Available at NS ticket machines and tourist information points.

- **Tips for Using Public Transport Like a Local:**

    - **Plan your journey:** Use journey planners like 9292.nl (website and app) to map your route, see real-time departures, and plan connections. This is what locals use!

    - **Check-in and Check-out diligently:** Always remember to check in at the start and check out at the end of each journey leg.

    - **Mind the peak hours:** Public transport can be crowded during rush hours (weekdays

7-9 am and 4-6 pm). If possible, travel outside these times for a more comfortable ride.

- **Listen to announcements:** Pay attention to announcements at stations and on vehicles for any delays or platform changes.

- **Ask for help if needed:** Dutch people are generally helpful and many speak excellent English. Don't hesitate to ask transport staff or fellow passengers for directions or assistance.

Local Transportation Apps: Your Digital Travel Assistants

In today's digital age, apps make navigating public transport even easier. Here are some must-have apps for getting around the Netherlands:

- **Must-Have Apps for Navigation, Ticketing, and Real-Time Updates:**

    - **9292 (pronounced "negen-twee-negen-twee"):** The ultimate journey planner for all Dutch public transport. It provides door-to-door travel advice, real-time departure information, disruptions, and even allows you to buy e-tickets for certain journeys. Available on both Android and [iOS](iOS).

- **NS App (Nederlandse Spoorwegen):** Specifically for train travel. Buy e-tickets, check train times, platform information, and get real-time updates on train journeys. Essential if you plan to travel by train a lot. Available on Android and [iOS](iOS).

- **Google Maps:** Reliable for general navigation, walking, cycling, and driving directions. Also integrates public transport information, although 9292 is more comprehensive for public transport within the Netherlands. Available on Android and [iOS](iOS).

- **Citymapper:** Excellent for urban navigation, especially in Amsterdam, Rotterdam, and The Hague. Provides real-time public transport information, cycling routes, and walking directions. Available on Android and [iOS](iOS).
- **Step-by-Step Guides for Using Key Transportation Apps:**

Let's take **9292** as an example, as it's the most comprehensive for public transport:

1. **Download and Install:** Get the 9292 app from your app store (links above).

2. **Enter Departure and Destination:** Open the app and in the journey planner, enter your starting point (e.g., "Amsterdam Centraal") and your destination (e.g., "Keukenhof Gardens").

You can use addresses, place names, or even just tap on the map.

3. **Choose Date and Time:** Set your desired departure or arrival time.

4. **View Journey Options:** The app will display various route options, often including train, bus, and tram combinations. It shows travel time, changes, and even estimated costs.

5. **Select a Route:** Choose the route that best suits you. Tap on a route for detailed step-by-step instructions.

6. **Real-time Information:** During your journey, the app updates with real-time information about delays or changes.

Bike Rentals and Cycling Routes: Pedal Your Way Through Paradise

Cycling is not just a mode of transport in the Netherlands; it's a way of life! With flat landscapes and extensive cycling paths, it's the perfect way to explore.

- **The Netherlands: A Cyclist's Dream Destination:**

The Netherlands is incredibly bike-friendly. You'll find dedicated cycle paths everywhere, often separate from roads and pedestrian paths. Traffic rules prioritize cyclists, making it safe and enjoyable. Many Dutch people cycle daily for commuting, errands, and leisure. Joining them on a bike is a fantastic way to experience the Dutch lifestyle and see more than you would on foot or by car.

- **Finding Bike Rental Services and Choosing the Right Bike:**

Bike rentals are widely available in cities and towns, especially near train stations and tourist areas.

- **Rental Shops:** Look for "Fietsverhuur" (bike rental) signs. Shops are plentiful, particularly in Amsterdam and other tourist hotspots. Good rental companies include **MacBike** (https://www.macbike.nl/en/) and **Discount Bike Rental** (https://www.discountbikerental.nl/). You can often book online or just walk in.

- **Hotel Rentals:** Many hotels offer bike rentals to guests, which can be very convenient.

- **Bike Sharing Systems:** Some cities have bike-sharing schemes, but these are less common than in some other European cities and might be less geared towards tourists for longer rentals.

- **Choosing the Right Bike:**
    - **"Omafiets" (Grandma Bike):** The classic Dutch bike – upright, comfortable, sturdy, often with backpedal brakes. Perfect for leisurely city cycling.
    - **Touring Bike:** Gears for hills (though the Netherlands is mostly flat!), lighter frame,

good for longer distances and countryside routes.

- **Electric Bike (E-bike):** Assisted pedaling, great if you want to cover more ground with less effort, or if you are not a regular cyclist.

- **Kids' Bikes and Child Seats:** Available for families.

- **Popular Cycling Routes and Scenic Trails:**

The Netherlands is crisscrossed with fantastic cycling routes.

- **City Cycling in Amsterdam:** Explore the canals, parks, and neighborhoods by bike. Follow canal rings, Vondelpark paths, or head to Amsterdam Noord by ferry and cycle through the IJ countryside.

- **Countryside Routes:**

    - **Tulip Route (Bollenstreek):** (Spring only) Cycle through vibrant tulip fields between Haarlem and Leiden.

    - **Windmill Route (Kinderdijk):** Cycle around the UNESCO World Heritage site of Kinderdijk windmills.

    - **National Park De Hoge Veluwe:** Cycle through forests,

heathland, and sand dunes within the national park (bikes are often included with park entry).

- **Coastal Routes:** Cycle along the North Sea coast, enjoying sea views and seaside towns.

- **Long-Distance Routes (LF Routes):** The Netherlands has a network of long-distance cycling routes (LF routes) marked with signs. Great for multi-day cycling trips. Website [Holland Cycling Routes](#) provides information and maps.

- **Cycling Safety Tips and Local Cycling Etiquette:**
    - **Use Cycle Paths:** Always use designated cycle paths (red or reddish-brown paths, often separated from roads).
    - **Traffic Rules:** Learn basic Dutch cycling traffic rules (right of way, hand signals). Cyclists have priority over cars in many situations, but be aware and cautious.
    - **Hand Signals:** Use hand signals to indicate turns and stops.
    - **Lights at Night:** Bike lights are mandatory at night and in poor visibility. Ensure your rental bike has working lights.

- **Lock Your Bike:** Bike theft is common, especially in cities. Always use a good quality lock and lock your bike to a fixed object.

- **Be Aware of Other Cyclists and Pedestrians:** Cycle at a reasonable speed and be mindful of others, especially in crowded areas.

- **"Bicycle Bell":** Use your bell to alert pedestrians or other cyclists when overtaking or approaching.

Car Rentals: Freedom to Explore at Your Own Pace

While public transport and cycling are excellent, renting a car can be beneficial for exploring more remote areas or for greater flexibility, especially if you plan to venture into the countryside extensively.

- **When to Consider Renting a Car in the Netherlands:**

    - **Exploring Rural Areas:** For reaching smaller villages, nature reserves, and areas with limited public transport access.

    - **Road Trips:** For scenic drives and exploring multiple regions at your own pace.

    - **Families with Young Children or Lots of Luggage:** For added convenience and comfort.

    - **Less City-Centric Travel:** If you plan to spend less time in major cities and more time in the countryside.

- **Car Rental Companies and Booking Tips:**

Major international car rental companies operate at Schiphol Airport and in major cities (e.g., Avis, Hertz, Europcar, Sixt). Dutch companies like **Enterprise Rent-A-Car** (https://www.enterprise.nl/en/home.html) are also good options.

- **Book in Advance:** Especially during peak season, book your car rental in advance online for better rates and availability. Websites like **Booking.com**, **Rentalcars.com**, or directly through company websites are good for comparisons and bookings.

- **Consider Car Size:** Dutch roads, especially in cities, can be narrow. A smaller car is often easier to maneuver and park.

- **Automatic vs. Manual:** Automatic cars are available but manual transmission is more common and often cheaper. Specify your preference when booking.

- **Insurance:** Ensure you have adequate car insurance coverage. Check what's included in the rental price and consider additional coverage for peace of mind.

- **Pick-up and Drop-off Location:** Airport rentals are convenient upon arrival/departure. City center locations are also available.
- **Driving Regulations, Parking, and Tolls:**
  - **Driving Side:** Drive on the right side of the road.
  - **Speed Limits:** Speed limits are in kilometers per hour (km/h). Typically, 50 km/h in urban areas, 80 km/h outside urban areas, and 100-130 km/h on highways (motorways). Speed limits are strictly enforced.
  - **Priority to Cyclists and Pedestrians:** Be extremely mindful of cyclists and

pedestrians, especially in cities. Give way to cyclists and pedestrians at crossings.

- **Traffic Signs:** Road signs are in Dutch, but international symbols are also used.

- **Parking:** Parking in city centers can be expensive and limited. Look for "Parkeergarage" (parking garage) signs. Street parking is often metered and can be paid via parking meters or parking apps (like **ParkMobile** or **Yellowbrick**). Pay attention to parking signs and restrictions to avoid fines.

- **Tolls:** The Netherlands has very few toll roads. You're unlikely to encounter tolls on standard routes. The Westerscheldetunnel and Kiltunnel are toll tunnels.

- **Scenic Road Trip Routes and Drives:**

    - **North Sea Coastal Route:** Drive along the scenic North Sea coast, stopping at beaches, dunes, and charming seaside towns.

    - **Afsluitdijk Drive:** Drive across the impressive 32 km long Afsluitdijk causeway, separating the IJsselmeer lake from the Wadden Sea.

    - **"Green Heart" Route:** Explore the rural "Green Heart" region between major cities, with polders, canals, and charming villages.

- **Southern Limburg Hills Route:** Discover the rolling hills and vineyards of South Limburg, a unique landscape in the Netherlands.

- **Transportation for Remote Areas and Countryside Exploration:**

While public transport reaches many towns, a car provides more flexibility for exploring truly remote areas. In very rural areas, bus services may be less frequent. Always check public transport schedules in advance if relying on buses in the countryside. Cycling is also a fantastic option for exploring rural areas at a slower pace.

Local Transportation Options

Besides public transport, cycling, and cars, here are a couple of other options:

- **Taxis and Ride-Sharing Services:**

    - **Taxis:** Readily available in cities, especially at train stations, airports, and taxi stands. Taxis are metered. Major taxi companies operate in cities.

    - **Ride-Sharing Apps:** Uber and Bolt operate in major Dutch cities. These can be convenient, especially for airport transfers or late-night travel. Download the apps (**Uber**, **Bolt**) and link your payment method before you arrive.

- **Water Taxis and Canal Boats in Amsterdam:**

    - **Water Taxis (Amsterdam):** A faster and more private way to travel on Amsterdam's canals than canal boats. Water taxis can be booked by phone or app (**Watertaxi Amsterdam** app). More expensive than public transport, but a unique experience.

    - **Canal Boats (Amsterdam):** While primarily for sightseeing, canal boats can also be used as a form of transport between certain points on the canals, especially if you're not in a hurry and want to enjoy the scenery. Some canal boat companies offer hop-on-hop-off services.

CHAPTER 3

MONEY MATTERS AND PRACTICALITIES

Currency Exchange Locations and Tips

The Netherlands uses the **Euro (€)**.

- **Understanding the Euro (€):**

The Euro is the currency of the Eurozone, including the Netherlands. Euro banknotes come in denominations of €5, €10, €20, €50, €100, €200, and €500 (though €500 notes are less common). Euro coins come in denominations of 1 cent, 2 cents, 5 cents, 10 cents, 20 cents, 50 cents, €1, and €2.

- **Best Places to Exchange Currency: Banks, Exchange Bureaus, ATMs:**
    - **ATMs (Cash Machines):** The most convenient and often best exchange rates. ATMs are widely available at airports, train stations, city centers, and bank branches. Look for ATMs of major Dutch banks like **ABN AMRO**, **ING**, or **Rabobank**. Ensure your bank card is enabled for international use and be aware of potential foreign transaction fees from your bank.
    - **Banks:** You *can* exchange currency at banks, but it's often less convenient and

may have less favorable exchange rates than ATMs. Bank branches with currency exchange services might be limited.

- **Exchange Bureaus (GWK Travelex, etc.):** Found at airports and major train stations. Convenient but often offer less competitive exchange rates and higher commission fees than ATMs. Compare rates before exchanging. **GWK Travelex** (https://www.gwktravelex.nl/en) is a common exchange bureau in the Netherlands.

- **Avoid exchanging currency at hotels or tourist traps:** These usually offer the worst exchange rates.

- **Using Credit and Debit Cards: Acceptance and Fees:**

    - **Credit and Debit Card Acceptance:** Credit and debit cards (Visa, Mastercard, American Express) are widely accepted in larger stores, hotels, restaurants, and tourist attractions, *especially in major cities*. However, in smaller shops, markets, cafes, and especially outside major cities, **card acceptance can be less common, and cash is often preferred or even the only option.** Dutch people often use debit cards (Maestro or V Pay).

- **"Pin" (Debit Card) Preference:** Dutch people heavily rely on debit cards (called "pinpas" in Dutch). You'll see signs saying "Pin Only" or "PIN" indicating debit card payment is preferred or the only option.

- **Contactless Payment:** Contactless payment with cards and mobile pay (Apple Pay, Google Pay) is increasingly common in the Netherlands.

- **Foreign Transaction Fees:** Check with your bank about foreign transaction fees for using your card abroad. Some cards have no foreign transaction fees, which can save you money. Consider getting a travel-friendly card with low or no foreign transaction fees before your trip.

- **Always have some cash:** It's wise to carry some Euro cash for smaller purchases, markets, tips, and places where cards might not be accepted.

Money Matters: Budgeting and Costs

The Netherlands can be moderately expensive, especially Amsterdam. Budgeting is key.

- **Average Daily Expenses for Different Travel Styles (Budget, Mid-Range, Luxury):**

These are *rough* estimates and can vary greatly depending on your spending habits and travel style:

- **Budget Traveler (€50-€80 per day):** Hostels (€25-€35/night), budget-friendly meals (street food, supermarket sandwiches, affordable cafes - €15-€25/day), free attractions and walking tours, local transport (OV-chipkaart).

- **Mid-Range Traveler (€100-€180 per day):** Mid-range hotels or Airbnb (€80-€150/night), restaurant meals (€30-€60/day), paid attractions, public transport and some bike rentals.

- **Luxury Traveler (€250+ per day):** Luxury hotels (€200+/night), fine dining restaurants (€80+/day), taxis, private tours, high-end shopping.
- **Tipping Etiquette in Restaurants, Cafes, and Services:**

Tipping is not as ingrained in Dutch culture as in some other countries (like the USA).

- **Restaurants and Cafes:** Service charges are usually included in the bill. Tipping is not obligatory, but it's common to round up the bill or leave a small tip (5-10%)

for good service, especially in restaurants. For exceptional service, you can tip more.

- **Cafes and Bars:** Rounding up the bill is common, or leaving small change.

- **Taxis:** Rounding up the fare is customary.

- **Hotels:** Tipping hotel staff (porters, housekeeping) is not expected but appreciated for good service.

- **Tours Guides:** Tipping tour guides is appreciated if you enjoyed the tour (5-10% is a guideline).

- **Saving Money on Accommodation, Food, and Activities:**
    - **Accommodation:**
        - **Hostels:** Dorm beds are the cheapest option, great for budget travelers and meeting people.
        - **Budget Hotels/Guesthouses:** Look outside the very city center for more affordable hotels.
        - **Airbnb/Apartment Rentals:** Can be cost-effective, especially for longer stays or groups.

- **Travel in Off-Peak Season:** Accommodation prices are significantly lower in autumn and winter.

- **Food:**

  - **Supermarkets:** Buy groceries for breakfast, lunch picnics, and snacks. Dutch supermarkets like **Albert Heijn**, **Jumbo**, and **Lidl** are widely available.

  - **Street Food and Markets:** Affordable and delicious options, especially for lunch. Try "haringhandels" (herring stands), "friteries" (fries shops), and markets like Albert Cuyp Market in Amsterdam.

- **Lunch Deals:** Many restaurants offer more affordable lunch menus compared to dinner.

- **Cook Your Own Meals:** If staying in an apartment with a kitchen, cooking some meals yourself can save a lot.

- **"Happy Hour" and "Daghap" (Dish of the Day):** Look for cafes and restaurants offering happy hour drink deals or "daghap" for budget-friendly set meals.

- **Activities:**

    - **Free Walking Tours:** Many cities offer free walking tours (tip-based). A great way to get oriented and see the main sights on a budget.

    - **Free Attractions:** Parks (like Vondelpark in Amsterdam), canals (walk along them), markets, and many churches are free to enter.

    - **Museum Passes:** If planning to visit many museums, consider city museum passes (like the **Amsterdam City Card**, **Rotterdam Welcome Card**, **The Hague Welcome Card**) or the **Museumkaart** (for residents and long-term visitors). These can offer cost savings if you use them extensively.

- **Free Ferry to Amsterdam Noord:** Take the free ferry from behind Amsterdam Centraal Station to Amsterdam Noord for city views and exploring a different part of Amsterdam.

- **Picnics in Parks:** Enjoy lunch picnics in parks instead of eating in restaurants every day.

Electricity and Plug Adapters

Stay powered up!

- **Voltage and Frequency in the Netherlands:**

The Netherlands uses **230V voltage** and **50Hz frequency**. This is standard in most of Europe. If your electronic devices are designed for 220-240V and 50/60Hz (common in Europe and many parts of Asia), you likely won't need a voltage converter. However, always check the voltage label on your devices. If it says "100-240V" or "110-240V," it's compatible. If it says only "110V" (common in North America for some older devices), you *might* need a voltage converter, but it's usually better to use devices that are compatible with 230V.

- **Plug Type and Adapter Requirements:**

The Netherlands uses **Type C and Type F power plugs**. These are the standard European 2-pin plugs. Type F is grounded, Type C is ungrounded, but they are compatible with each other.

- **Adapter Needed:** If your devices have plugs that are not Type C or Type F (e.g., if you are coming from the UK (Type G), USA (Type A or B), Australia (Type I)), you will **need a plug adapter**.

- **Where to Buy Adapters:**
  - **Before you travel:** Buy adapters online (Amazon, travel websites) or at electronics stores before your trip – often cheaper and more convenient.
  - **At Airports:** Airport shops usually sell travel adapters, but they can be more expensive.
  - **In the Netherlands:** You can buy adapters at electronics stores (like **MediaMarkt**), department stores, and some tourist shops in the Netherlands, but it's

easier to have one ready when you arrive.

- **USB Charging:** Many hotels and cafes have USB charging ports available, which can be useful for phones and tablets without needing an adapter (if you have a USB cable).

Internet and Communication

Staying connected is easy in the Netherlands.

- **Staying Connected: Mobile Data, SIM Cards, and Wi-Fi:**
  - **Mobile Data Roaming:** Check with your mobile provider about international roaming plans. Roaming can

be convenient but often expensive. Within the EU, roaming charges are generally eliminated for EU citizens, but check for your specific plan if you are from outside the EU.

- **Local SIM Cards:** A cost-effective option for longer stays or heavy data use. You can buy prepaid SIM cards from Dutch mobile providers like **KPN**, **Vodafone**, or **T-Mobile**. Shops of these providers are found in city centers and shopping malls. You can also often buy SIM cards at phone shops or even some supermarkets. You'll need an unlocked phone to use a local SIM card.

- **Wi-Fi:** Free Wi-Fi is widely available in cafes, restaurants, hotels, and some public spaces throughout the Netherlands.
- **Public Wi-Fi Availability: Locations and Security Tips:**
  - **Locations:** Many cafes, restaurants, libraries, train stations, and even some trams and buses offer free Wi-Fi. Look for Wi-Fi network names like "Free Wi-Fi," "Public Wi-Fi," or networks named after the establishment.
  - **Security Tips:**
    - **Use VPN (Virtual Private Network):** For enhanced security,

especially when using public Wi-Fi, use a VPN app on your phone or laptop.

- **HTTPS Websites:** Ensure websites you visit (especially for sensitive information like banking) use "HTTPS" (look for the padlock icon in the browser address bar).

- **Avoid Sensitive Transactions on Public Wi-Fi:** Be cautious about doing online banking or making purchases on public Wi-Fi. Use mobile data or a secure network for sensitive transactions.

- **Disable Automatic Connection:** Disable automatic Wi-Fi connection on your devices to prevent automatically connecting to unsecured networks.

- **Using Your Phone in the Netherlands: Roaming and Local Plans:**

    - **Roaming:** If you choose to use your existing mobile plan's roaming, activate international roaming with your provider before you travel. Check roaming charges and data allowances to avoid unexpected bills.

- **Local SIM Card:** If you opt for a local SIM card, you can purchase prepaid plans with data, calls, and texts. You can often buy these at provider shops with just your passport for identification. Activating the SIM and setting up data can usually be done easily by following instructions provided with the SIM card.

- **Emergency Calls:** The emergency number in the Netherlands (and throughout the EU) is **112**. You can dial 112 for police, fire, or ambulance in emergencies, even without a SIM card or credit.

CHAPTER 4

AMSTERDAM - THE ICONIC CAPITAL

Must-See Areas in Amsterdam

Amsterdam is a city best explored neighborhood by neighborhood, each with its own distinct character and appeal.

- **The Canal Ring (Grachtengordel): Jordaan, Herengracht, Keizersgracht, Prinsengracht**

The Canal Ring, a UNESCO World Heritage site, is the postcard-perfect Amsterdam you've dreamed of. Imagine layers of elegant canals – **Herengracht (Gentlemen's Canal), Keizersgracht (Emperor's Canal), Prinsengracht (Prince's Canal)** – curving gracefully around the city center, lined with stunning canal houses from the Golden Age. Walking or cycling along these canals is a must-do. Take a canal cruise to truly appreciate the architecture from the water level.

Jordaan, once a working-class neighborhood, is now a charming, bohemian district with narrow streets, boutique shops, art galleries, and cozy "brown cafes" (traditional Dutch pubs). It's perfect for wandering, getting lost in its lanes, and soaking up the relaxed atmosphere. To get to Jordaan, simply walk west from Amsterdam Centraal Station or Dam Square, crossing over Prinsengracht canal.

Practical Tip: For a classic Amsterdam experience, rent a bike and cycle along the Canal Ring. Many rental shops are located near Centraal Station. Alternatively, join a guided walking tour of the Jordaan to discover its hidden stories and local gems. Consider a canal cruise starting from Damrak or near Centraal Station for an iconic water-level view.

- **De Pijp: Vibrant Neighborhood with Markets and Cafes**

South of the city center, **De Pijp** is a lively, multicultural neighborhood known for its bustling **Albert Cuyp Market**, a daily street market where you can find everything from fresh produce and cheese to clothing and souvenirs. De Pijp is also packed with trendy cafes, restaurants serving cuisines from around the globe, and hip bars. It's a great place to experience Amsterdam's contemporary, diverse vibe.

Practical Tip: Visit Albert Cuyp Market during the day (it's open Monday-Saturday) for a true local experience and some delicious street food. De Pijp is easily reached by tram lines from Centraal Station or Dam Square. Explore the Sarphatipark, a green oasis within De Pijp, for a relaxing break from the market buzz.

- **Jordaan: Historic Charm and Boutique Shops**

While mentioned within the Canal Ring, **Jordaan** deserves its own spotlight. This former working-class area has transformed into one of Amsterdam's most beloved neighborhoods, retaining its historic charm with picturesque canals, narrow streets, and gabled houses. Jordaan is now known for its independent boutiques, art galleries, antique shops, and traditional "brown cafes." It's a perfect place for leisurely strolls and discovering unique finds.

Practical Tip: Wander through the Nine Streets (De Negen Straatjes) within Jordaan for unique boutique shopping. Enjoy a traditional Dutch lunch at a "brown cafe" in Jordaan – try Café Papeneiland or Café 't Smalle for authentic atmosphere. Take a guided Jordaan walking tour to learn about its fascinating history.

- **Museumplein: Culture Hub with World-Class Museums**

Museumplein (Museum Square) is Amsterdam's cultural heart, home to three world-renowned museums: the **Rijksmuseum**, the **Van Gogh Museum**, and the **Stedelijk Museum** (modern art). The square itself is a spacious public area perfect for relaxing, picnicking, and taking photos with the iconic "IAMSTERDAM" letters (though these are sometimes removed for political reasons, check local updates).

Practical Tip: Museumplein can get very busy, especially on weekends and holidays. Book museum tickets online in advance to skip the ticket lines. Arrive early in the morning to avoid the biggest crowds. Combine museum visits with relaxing in the square or enjoying a picnic lunch. Museumplein is easily accessible by tram from Centraal Station or Dam Square.

- **Red Light District (De Wallen): History and Responsible Exploration**

The **Red Light District (De Wallen)** is Amsterdam's most notorious and historically significant area. It's known for its canals, historic buildings, and, of course, its window prostitution. It's important to approach this area with respect and awareness. During the day, it's a historic neighborhood with the **Oude Kerk (Old Church)**, Amsterdam's oldest building, at its heart. At night, it transforms into a vibrant (and sometimes overwhelming) entertainment district.

Practical Tip: Explore the Red Light District during the daytime to appreciate its historic architecture and canals. If you visit at night, be respectful, avoid taking photos of sex workers without consent, and be aware of pickpockets and crowds. Consider a guided walking tour that focuses on the history and social context of the Red Light District for a more informed perspective. The Red Light

District is located east of Dam Square, easily walkable.

- **Vondelpark: Amsterdam's Green Oasis**

Vondelpark is Amsterdam's largest and most beloved park, a green lung in the city center. It's a perfect escape for relaxation, picnics, cycling, walking, or simply enjoying nature. In summer, it hosts free open-air theater and concerts. You'll find playgrounds, cafes, and even a rose garden within the park.

Practical Tip: Rent a bike and cycle through Vondelpark. Enjoy a picnic lunch in the park. Check the Vondelpark Open Air Theatre schedule in summer for free performances. Vondelpark is located south of the city center, easily accessible by tram or bike from Museumplein or Leidseplein.

Historical Landmarks and Monuments in Amsterdam

Amsterdam's history is etched into its landmarks and monuments, each telling a story of the city's rich past.

- **Anne Frank House: A Powerful and Moving Experience**

The **Anne Frank House** is a profoundly moving museum located in the canal house where Anne Frank and her family hid from Nazi persecution during World War II. Visiting the secret annex where Anne wrote her famous diary is an unforgettable and deeply impactful experience. It's a reminder of history and a testament to the resilience of the human spirit.

Practical Tip: Book tickets online *well in advance*, as tickets often sell out weeks or even months ahead, especially during peak season. Arrive at your booked time slot to avoid long queues. The museum is located on Prinsengracht canal in the city center. Allow at least 1.5-2 hours for your visit to fully absorb the experience. Photography is not allowed inside the secret annex to preserve the atmosphere.

- **Royal Palace of Amsterdam (Koninklijk Paleis Amsterdam)**

Located on Dam Square, the **Royal Palace** is one of three palaces in the Netherlands which are at the disposal of the monarch by law. It was originally built as Amsterdam's City Hall in the 17th century, during the Dutch Golden Age, and later became a royal palace. It's a grand building filled with opulent interiors, art, and historical significance. You can take a tour to explore its state rooms and learn about its history.

Practical Tip: Check the Royal Palace's website (https://www.paleisamsterdam.nl/en/) for opening hours and to book tickets online. Allow about 1-1.5 hours for a visit. Combine your palace visit with exploring Dam Square and nearby attractions.

- **Rijksmuseum: Dutch Masters and Art History**

The **Rijksmuseum** is the Netherlands' national museum, housing an unparalleled collection of Dutch Masters from the Golden Age, including Rembrandt's "The Night Watch," Vermeer's "The Milkmaid," and works by Frans Hals and Jan Steen. Beyond paintings, it also showcases Dutch history, sculptures, decorative arts, and Asian art. It's a must-visit for art lovers and anyone interested in Dutch culture and history.

Practical Tip: Book tickets online in advance to avoid queues. The Rijksmuseum is vast; plan your visit based on your interests (Golden Age art, Dutch history, etc.). Allow at least 3-4 hours, or even a full day, to explore it properly. Audio guides are available. The Rijksmuseum is located on Museumplein.

- **Van Gogh Museum: Immersive Art Experience**

The **Van Gogh Museum** is dedicated to the life and works of Vincent van Gogh, one of the most famous and influential figures in Western art history. It houses the world's largest collection of Van Gogh's paintings and drawings, tracing his artistic journey and turbulent life. It's an immersive experience for art enthusiasts and those wanting to understand Van Gogh's genius.

Practical Tip: Book tickets online in advance, as time slots are required and sell out quickly. The museum is located on Museumplein, very close to the Rijksmuseum. Allow 2-3 hours for your visit. Audio guides are highly recommended to enhance your understanding of Van Gogh's art and life.

- **Dam Square: The Heart of Amsterdam**

Dam Square is the central square of Amsterdam, a bustling hub surrounded by significant buildings: the Royal Palace, **Nieuwe Kerk (New Church)**, **Madame Tussauds**, and the **National Monument**. It's a lively square, often filled with street performers, tourists, and pigeons. Dam Square is the historical and symbolic heart of Amsterdam.

Practical Tip: Dam Square is a central meeting point and a good starting point for exploring Amsterdam. Visit the Royal Palace and Nieuwe Kerk located on the square. Be aware of pickpockets in crowded areas. Dam Square is easily accessible by tram from Centraal Station.

- **Westerkerk: Iconic Church with Panoramic Views**

Westerkerk (Western Church) is Amsterdam's tallest church and an iconic landmark, easily recognizable by its tall spire topped with the Imperial Crown of Austria. You can climb the **Westertoren (Western Tower)** for panoramic views over Amsterdam's canals and rooftops (seasonal opening, ticket required). The church itself is a beautiful example of Dutch Renaissance architecture. Anne Frank mentioned the Westertoren bells in her diary.

Practical Tip: Climbing the Westertoren is a must for stunning city views, but tickets are limited and often sell out, book in advance or arrive early. Check the Westerkerk website (https://www.westerkerk.nl/en/) for tower opening times and ticket information. The Westerkerk is located near the Anne Frank House, in the Jordaan area.

- **Oude Kerk (Old Church): Amsterdam's Oldest Building**

The **Oude Kerk (Old Church)**, located in the heart of the Red Light District, is Amsterdam's oldest building, dating back to the 13th century. It's a fascinating contrast – a historic church surrounded by the city's most libertine district. Inside, you'll find beautiful stained glass windows, wooden ceilings, and historical artifacts. It's a place of history, art, and reflection in an unexpected setting.

Practical Tip: Visit the Oude Kerk to experience its unique atmosphere and explore its history. Combine your visit with a walk through the Red Light District during the daytime to appreciate the contrast. Check the Oude Kerk website (https://www.oudekerk.nl/en/) for opening hours and any special exhibitions.

Museums in Amsterdam: A Cultural Feast

Amsterdam is a museum lover's paradise, offering a vast array of museums covering art, history, science, and unique Dutch experiences.

- **Rijksmuseum, Van Gogh Museum, Anne Frank House (Detailed Guides)**

These three museums are so significant they deserve extra attention. (Detailed guides are already provided above in "Historical Landmarks and Monuments"). Remember to book tickets in advance for all three to guarantee entry and save time.

- **Stedelijk Museum: Modern and Contemporary Art**

The **Stedelijk Museum** is Amsterdam's premier museum for modern and contemporary art and design. It houses an impressive collection of works by artists like Picasso, Matisse, Mondrian, and Warhol, spanning movements from early modernism to today's cutting-edge art. If you are interested in 20th and 21st-century art, this museum is a must.

Practical Tip: Book tickets online in advance. The Stedelijk Museum is located on Museumplein, close to the Rijksmuseum and Van Gogh Museum, making it easy to combine visits. Allow 2-3 hours for your visit. Check their website (https://www.stedelijk.nl/en) for current exhibitions and events.

- **Hermitage Amsterdam: Branch of the St. Petersburg Hermitage**

Hermitage Amsterdam is a branch museum of the famous Hermitage Museum in St. Petersburg, Russia. It hosts temporary exhibitions showcasing treasures from the Hermitage collection in Russia, often focusing on Russian history and culture, as well as Dutch-Russian connections. The museum is housed in a beautiful historic building on the Amstel River. (Note: Due to current geopolitical situations, exhibitions and the museum's focus may be subject to change. Check their website for the most up-to-date information).

Practical Tip: Check the Hermitage Amsterdam website (https://hermitage.nl/en/) for current exhibitions and opening hours. It's located on the Amstel River, a short walk from Waterlooplein. Allow 1.5-2 hours for a visit, depending on the exhibition.

- **NEMO Science Museum: Interactive Science for All Ages**

NEMO Science Museum is a fantastic interactive science museum, perfect for families and anyone curious about science and technology. It features hands-on exhibits on topics like physics, chemistry, biology, and the human brain. Kids (and adults!) can conduct experiments, learn about scientific principles, and have fun while exploring. The museum is housed in a distinctive green copper-clad building shaped like a ship, near Amsterdam Centraal Station.

Practical Tip: Book tickets online, especially if visiting during school holidays or weekends. NEMO is very popular with families. Allow at least 3-4 hours, or even a full day, especially if you're visiting with children. The rooftop terrace of NEMO offers great city views and is free to access even without a museum ticket. NEMO is a short walk from Amsterdam Centraal Station.

- **Scheepvaartmuseum (National Maritime Museum): Dutch Naval History**

The **Scheepvaartmuseum (National Maritime Museum)** delves into the Netherlands' rich maritime history, from the Golden Age seafaring to modern shipping. It features historical ships (including a replica of a Dutch East Indiaman), maritime artifacts, interactive exhibits, and stories of Dutch exploration and naval power. It's a fascinating museum for those interested in boats, ships, and maritime adventures.

Practical Tip: The Scheepvaartmuseum is located near Amsterdam Centraal Station, a short walk or tram ride away. Allow 2-3 hours for your visit. Explore the replica ship docked outside and the interactive exhibits inside.

- **Amsterdam Museum: History of the City**

The **Amsterdam Museum** tells the story of Amsterdam's history, from its humble beginnings as a small fishing village to the vibrant metropolis it is today. Exhibits cover Amsterdam's social, cultural, and economic development over centuries, using artifacts, paintings, and interactive displays. It's a great museum to understand the city's evolution and identity.

Practical Tip: The Amsterdam Museum is located in a former orphanage, close to the Begijnhof. Allow 2-3 hours for a comprehensive visit. It's a good museum to visit early in your trip to gain context for your Amsterdam exploration. Check their website (https://www.amsterdammuseum.nl/en) for opening hours and current exhibitions.

- **Houseboat Museum: Experience Life on a Canal Boat**

For a unique and quirky experience, visit the **Houseboat Museum**. It's a real, former houseboat converted into a small museum, offering a glimpse into life on Amsterdam's canals. You can explore the living spaces, learn about the history of houseboats, and imagine what it's like to live on the water in Amsterdam.

Practical Tip: The Houseboat Museum is a small, intimate museum, perfect for a short, unique visit. It's located on Prinsengracht canal in the Jordaan area. Allow about 30-45 minutes for your visit. It's a fun and offbeat attraction, especially if you're curious about Amsterdam's canal lifestyle. Check their website (https://www.houseboatmuseum.nl/) for exact location and opening times.

Free Tourist Attractions in Amsterdam

Amsterdam doesn't have to break the bank. There are plenty of fantastic free things to see and do.

- **Walking Tours of the Canal Ring and Jordaan**

Simply walking along the Canal Ring and through the Jordaan is a free and wonderful way to experience Amsterdam's beauty and atmosphere. You can create your own walking route or join a **free walking tour** (tip-based). Many free walking tours start from Dam Square or Centraal Station and cover the main highlights of the city center,

112

including the Canal Ring and Jordaan. **Sandeman's New Europe** (https://www.neweuropetours.eu/amsterdam/en/home) is a popular provider of free walking tours.

Practical Tip: Wear comfortable shoes for walking. Pick up a free city map from a tourist information center or download a map app on your phone. Join a free walking tour at the start of your Amsterdam visit to get an overview of the city and its main attractions. Remember to tip your guide if you enjoy the tour.

- **Vondelpark Exploration and Relaxation**

Spending time in **Vondelpark** is completely free. You can walk, cycle, picnic, people-watch, enjoy street performers, or simply relax by the ponds and greenery. It's Amsterdam's free outdoor playground for everyone.

Practical Tip: Bring a picnic blanket and snacks to enjoy a relaxing afternoon in Vondelpark. Rent a bike and cycle through the park's paths. Check for free events and performances happening in the park during your visit, especially in summer.

- **Albert Cuyp Market: Local Market Experience**

Wandering through **Albert Cuyp Market** is free, and soaking up the atmosphere is an experience in itself. While you'll be tempted to buy delicious food and souvenirs, simply Browse the stalls, observing the lively market scene, and people-watching is a free and engaging activity.

Practical Tip: Visit Albert Cuyp Market in the morning or early afternoon for the best atmosphere and selection of goods. Even if you're on a budget, you can sample some affordable street food snacks at the market. Practice your Dutch by haggling (politely!) for better prices.

- **Free Ferry to Amsterdam Noord: Views and Industrial Charm**

Take the **free ferry from behind Amsterdam Centraal Station to Amsterdam Noord**. This ferry ride across the IJ waterway offers fantastic **free** views of Amsterdam's skyline and harbor. Amsterdam Noord is a former industrial area that has transformed into a creative and cultural hub with street art, trendy cafes, and unique venues like the **NDSM Wharf** (also mentioned below as a hidden gem).

Practical Tip: The free ferries depart frequently from behind Centraal Station (look for signs for "IJ-veer"). Take the ferry to NDSM Wharf to explore the creative area, street art, and cafes. Cycle around Amsterdam Noord to discover its parks, waterfront areas, and different atmosphere compared to the city center.

Paid Tourist Attractions in Amsterdam

For those willing to spend a bit, Amsterdam offers some truly iconic and memorable paid attractions.

- **Canal Cruises: Iconic Amsterdam Experience**

A **canal cruise** is arguably the most iconic Amsterdam experience. Gliding along the canals by boat provides a unique perspective on the city's architecture, canal houses, and bridges. Various canal cruise companies operate from different locations (Damrak, near Centraal Station, Leidseplein), offering different types of cruises: open boat, covered boat, evening cruises, themed cruises.

Practical Tip: Book canal cruise tickets online in advance, especially during peak season, to secure your spot and sometimes get discounts. Consider an evening canal cruise for a romantic experience with illuminated bridges and canal houses. Choose a smaller, open boat for a more intimate experience. Many cruises offer audio guides in multiple languages.

- **Heineken Experience: Brewery Tour and Tasting**

The **Heineken Experience** is a popular interactive museum and tour located in Heineken's former brewery. It takes you through the history of Heineken beer, the brewing process, and of course, includes beer tastings. It's a fun and engaging experience, especially for beer enthusiasts.

Practical Tip: Book tickets online in advance to avoid queues. The Heineken Experience is located in De Pijp neighborhood. Allow 2-3 hours for the tour and tasting. It's a popular attraction, so be prepared for crowds, especially during peak hours. Make sure you are of legal drinking age to participate in the beer tasting.

- **ARTIS Amsterdam Royal Zoo: Wildlife and Nature**

ARTIS Amsterdam Royal Zoo is one of the oldest zoos in Europe, located in the heart of Amsterdam. It's home to a wide variety of animals from around the world, as well as an aquarium, planetarium, and botanical gardens. It's a great attraction for families, animal lovers, and anyone seeking a green escape within the city.

Practical Tip: Book tickets online to save time and sometimes get discounts. ARTIS is a large zoo; allow at least 3-4 hours, or a full day, to explore it thoroughly. Check the ARTIS website (https://www.artis.nl/en/) for feeding times and special events. ARTIS is located east of the city center, reachable by tram.

- **Madame Tussauds Amsterdam: Wax Figures and Entertainment**

Madame Tussauds Amsterdam is a wax museum featuring lifelike wax figures of celebrities, historical figures, and Dutch icons. It's an entertaining and interactive attraction where you can take photos with your favorite "celebrities." It's located on Dam Square, making it a central stop in your Amsterdam exploration.

Practical Tip: Book tickets online in advance to save time and money. Madame Tussauds is located right on Dam Square, easy to combine with other Dam Square attractions. Allow 1-2 hours for your visit. It's a fun and lighthearted attraction, especially for families and pop culture enthusiasts.

- **A'DAM Lookout: Panoramic City Views and Thrill Rides**

A'DAM Lookout is an observation deck in Amsterdam Noord, offering unparalleled **360-degree panoramic views** of Amsterdam's skyline, canals, and harbor. Located in the A'DAM Tower, it also features thrill rides like "Over The Edge" (Europe's highest swing) for adrenaline junkies, as well as restaurants and bars with amazing views.

Practical Tip: Book tickets online to guarantee entry and sometimes get discounts. Take the free ferry from behind Centraal Station to Amsterdam Noord to reach A'DAM Lookout. Consider visiting at sunset for breathtaking views. If you're brave, try the "Over The Edge" swing. Allow 1.5-2 hours for your visit, including enjoying the views and potentially a drink or snack at the bar. Check the A'DAM Lookout website (https://www.adamlookout.com/) for opening hours and ticket options.

Off the Beaten Paths and Hidden Gems in Amsterdam

Venture beyond the main tourist trails to discover Amsterdam's hidden charms and local secrets.

- **Begijnhof: Serene Courtyard and Hidden History**

The **Begijnhof** is a hidden courtyard in the heart of Amsterdam, a tranquil oasis of peace and history. It was originally a beguinage, a community of unmarried religious women (beguines). It features historic houses, a hidden church, and a sense of serenity that feels miles away from the city bustle. It's a beautiful and peaceful escape.

Practical Tip: The Begijnhof is free to enter, but be respectful of the quiet atmosphere. It's located just off Spui square, easily missed if you don't know where to look – look for a discreet entrance gate. Visit during quieter hours (early morning or late afternoon) to fully appreciate the tranquility. Don't miss House No. 34, one of Amsterdam's oldest wooden houses.

- **NDSM Wharf: Creative Hub and Street Art Scene**

NDSM Wharf (NDSM-werf) is a former shipyard in Amsterdam Noord that has been transformed into a vibrant **creative and cultural hub**. It's filled with street art, graffiti, artist studios, trendy cafes, restaurants in repurposed shipping containers, and unique events. It's a raw, edgy, and alternative side of Amsterdam, a stark contrast to the polished city center.

Practical Tip: Take the free ferry from behind Centraal Station to NDSM Wharf. Explore the street art and graffiti – it's constantly changing. Enjoy a drink or meal at one of the trendy cafes or restaurants. Check for events and festivals happening at NDSM Wharf during your visit. Rent a bike in Amsterdam Noord and cycle around the area.

- **Hortus Botanicus Amsterdam: Botanical Gardens and Tranquility**

Hortus Botanicus Amsterdam is one of the oldest botanical gardens in the world, a peaceful oasis in the city center. It features diverse plant collections from around the globe, greenhouses with tropical plants, a butterfly garden, and a serene atmosphere. It's a perfect escape for nature lovers and those seeking tranquility.

Practical Tip: Tickets are required for Hortus Botanicus. It's located in the Plantage neighborhood, east of the city center. Allow 2-3 hours to explore the gardens thoroughly. Enjoy a coffee or lunch at the Hortus Cafe within the gardens. Check their website (https://www.dehortus.nl/en/) for opening hours and events.

- **Electric Ladyland Museum: Fluorescent Art and Psychedelic Experience**

The **Electric Ladyland Museum** is a truly unique and quirky museum dedicated to fluorescent art. It's a small, basement museum where you'll experience art that glows under blacklights, creating a psychedelic and immersive environment. It's a fun and unusual attraction for those seeking something different and offbeat.

Practical Tip: Tickets are required for Electric Ladyland. It's a small, intimate museum, located in the Jordaan area. Allow about 1 hour for your visit. It's a very unique and photo-worthy experience.

- **Explore the Nine Streets (De Negen Straatjes): Unique Boutiques and Cafes**

The Nine Streets (De Negen Straatjes), located within the Jordaan and Canal Ring, are nine charming streets crisscrossing the canals, filled with **independent boutiques, vintage shops, designer stores, art galleries,**

and cozy cafes. It's a shopper's paradise for unique finds and a great area for leisurely Browse and cafe hopping.

Practical Tip: Dedicate a few hours to wander through the Nine Streets, Browse shops and stopping at cafes. It's a great place to find unique souvenirs, Dutch design items, and vintage clothing. Combine your Nine Streets exploration with exploring the wider Jordaan neighborhood.

Fun Places and Parks in Amsterdam

Amsterdam offers plenty of fun and green spaces for leisure and recreation.

- **Vondelpark: Amsterdam's Largest Park**

(Already described above in "Must-See Areas"). Vondelpark is not just a park, it's a destination in itself, offering diverse activities and relaxation.

- **Westerpark: Trendy Park with Markets and Events**

Westerpark is a trendy park in western Amsterdam, known for its **Westergasfabriek**, a former gasworks complex that has been transformed into a cultural and event space. Westerpark hosts markets (like Sunday Market), festivals, food events, cafes, restaurants, and creative businesses. It's a vibrant and hip park, popular with locals.

Practical Tip: Check the Westerpark website or local event listings to see if there are markets or events happening during your visit, especially on weekends. Explore the Westergasfabriek buildings and their cafes and shops. Westerpark is located west of the city center, reachable by bus or tram.

- **Rembrandtpark: Family-Friendly Park with Playgrounds and Animals**

Rembrandtpark is a large, family-friendly park in western Amsterdam, less touristy than Vondelpark. It features playgrounds, petting zoos, canals, walking paths, and green spaces. It's a great park for families with children, offering space to run around, play, and enjoy nature.

Practical Tip: Rembrandtpark is ideal for families with kids. Let children enjoy the playgrounds and petting zoos. Bring a picnic or enjoy a snack at a park cafe. Rembrandtpark is located in western

Amsterdam, slightly further from the city center, but reachable by bus or tram.

- **ARTIS Amsterdam Royal Zoo: Wildlife Encounters**

(Already described above in "Paid Tourist Attractions"). ARTIS Zoo is not just a zoo, but also a beautiful park-like setting with gardens and historical buildings, offering a fun and educational experience for all ages.

- **NEMO Science Museum: Interactive Exhibits for Kids and Adults**

(Already described above in "Museums in Amsterdam"). NEMO Science Museum is not just educational, but also a fun and interactive place for both children and adults to explore science and technology.

CHAPTER 5

BEYOND AMSTERDAM - EXPLORING THE NETHERLANDS

Must-See Areas Outside Amsterdam

Venture beyond Amsterdam to discover the diverse regions and cities of the Netherlands, each with its own unique character.

- **The Hague (Den Haag): Royal City and International Hub**

The Hague (Den Haag) is the political heart of the Netherlands, the seat of the Dutch parliament (**Binnenhof**) and home to international organizations like the **International Court of Justice (Peace Palace)**. It's a sophisticated city with royal palaces, grand boulevards, excellent museums (**Mauritshuis, Escher in Het Paleis, Gemeentemuseum Den Haag**), and the seaside resort of **Scheveningen Beach** nearby.

Practical Tip: Take a guided tour of the Binnenhof. Visit the Mauritshuis to see Vermeer's "Girl with a Pearl Earring." Explore the Peace Palace and learn about international law. Spend a day at Scheveningen Beach, enjoying the pier, beach, and sea views. The Hague is easily reached by train from Amsterdam (approx. 30-40 minutes).

- **Rotterdam: Modern Architecture and Vibrant Port City**

Rotterdam is a city of striking **modern architecture**, rebuilt after being heavily bombed during WWII. It's known for its innovative buildings like the **Cube**

Houses, **Markthal**, and **Erasmus Bridge**. Rotterdam is also a bustling port city with a vibrant cultural scene, museums (**Museum Boijmans Van Beuningen, Maritime Museum Rotterdam**), and a dynamic energy.

Practical Tip: Take an architectural walking tour or bike tour of Rotterdam to appreciate its modern buildings. Visit the Cube Houses and Markthal. Go up the Euromast for panoramic city views. Explore the harbor area and consider a harbor cruise. Rotterdam is easily reached by train from Amsterdam (approx. 40-60 minutes).

- **Utrecht: Medieval Canals and Dom Tower**

Utrecht is a charming city with a beautiful **medieval city center** and unique **wharf cellars (werfkelders)** along its canals.

The **Dom Tower**, the tallest church tower in the Netherlands, dominates the skyline and offers fantastic city views. Utrecht has a relaxed and student-friendly atmosphere, with cozy cafes, restaurants, and shops.

Practical Tip: Climb the Dom Tower for panoramic views of Utrecht and the surrounding area (guided tours only, book in advance). Explore the wharf cellars along the Oudegracht canal, now housing cafes and restaurants. Visit the Centraal Museum to learn about Utrecht's history and art. Utrecht is easily reached by train from Amsterdam (approx. 25-30 minutes).

- **Delft: Delftware Pottery and Historic Charm**

Delft is a picturesque city famous for its **Delftware pottery (Delfts Blauw)**, the blue and white ceramics. It has a charming historic center with canals, the **Nieuwe Kerk (New Church)** where the Dutch royal family is buried, and the **Oude Kerk (Old Church)**. Visit a Delftware factory to see how this iconic pottery is made.

Practical Tip: Visit a Delftware factory like **Royal Delft** (https://www.royaldelft.com/) or **De Delftse Pauw** to see pottery being made and buy authentic Delftware. Explore the Markt square and Nieuwe Kerk. Delft is easily reached by train from The Hague or Rotterdam (approx. 10-15 minutes from each).

- **Leiden: University City and Botanical Gardens**

Leiden is a historic university city, home to the oldest university in the

Netherlands. It has a charming city center with canals, historic buildings, and museums, including the **Rijksmuseum van Oudheden (National Museum of Antiquities)** and the **Hortus Botanicus Leiden**, one of the oldest botanical gardens in Europe. Leiden has a lively student atmosphere and a rich history.

Practical Tip: Visit the Hortus Botanicus Leiden, one of the oldest botanical gardens in Europe. Explore the Rijksmuseum van Oudheden for ancient artifacts. Wander through the historic city center and canals. Leiden is easily reached by train from The Hague or Amsterdam (approx. 15-20 minutes from each).

- **Haarlem: Historic City near the Coast**

Haarlem is a historic city located close to the North Sea coast, often considered a smaller, more relaxed version of Amsterdam. It has a beautiful **Grote Markt (Main Square)** with the **Grote Kerk (St. Bavo Church)**, excellent museums (**Frans Hals Museum, Teylers Museum**), and a charming city center. It's also a gateway to the beach resort of **Zandvoort aan Zee**.

Practical Tip: Visit the Grote Markt and Grote Kerk. Explore the Frans Hals Museum for Dutch Golden Age art. Take a day trip to Zandvoort Beach, easily reached by train or bus from Haarlem. Haarlem is easily reached by train from Amsterdam (approx. 15-20 minutes).

- **Giethoorn: "Venice of the Netherlands" - Car-Free Village**

Giethoorn is a fairytale-like village known as the "Venice of the Netherlands." It's famous for its **canals, thatched-roof houses, and car-free center**. The best way to explore Giethoorn is by boat – rent a "whisper boat" (electric boat) or take a canal tour. It's a tranquil and idyllic escape.

Practical Tip: Rent a "whisper boat" to explore Giethoorn's canals at your own pace. Take a guided canal tour to learn about the village's history and culture. Walk or cycle around the village (outside the car-free center). Giethoorn is best reached by car or bus from nearby train stations (like Steenwijk). It can get crowded, especially in peak season; visit early morning or late afternoon for a quieter experience.

- **Zaanse Schans: Windmills and Traditional Crafts**

Zaanse Schans is a living museum village showcasing traditional Dutch windmills, crafts, and wooden houses. It's a picturesque area where you can see working windmills, watch cheese-making demonstrations, clog making, and explore traditional Dutch life. It's a popular day trip from Amsterdam to experience Dutch heritage.

Practical Tip: Zaanse Schans is easily reached by bus from Amsterdam Centraal Station (Bus 391). Explore the windmills, cheese factory, clog workshop, and wooden houses. Consider taking a boat trip on the Zaan River for different views of the windmills. It can get crowded with tourists; visit early morning or late afternoon for a less crowded experience.

- **Keukenhof Gardens (Spring Only): Tulip Paradise**

Keukenhof Gardens, open for only a few weeks in spring (typically late March to mid-May), is a world-famous flower garden showcasing millions of tulips, daffodils, hyacinths, and other spring flowers in breathtaking displays. It's a true tulip paradise and a must-visit if you are in the Netherlands during tulip season.

Practical Tip: Keukenhof is only open for a limited time in spring; check the official website (https://keukenhof.nl/en/) for exact opening dates each year. Book tickets online in advance, as tickets often sell out, especially on weekends and holidays. Keukenhof is best reached by bus from Schiphol Airport or Leiden Centraal Station. It can get very crowded; arrive early in the morning or late afternoon for a slightly less crowded experience.

- **Kinderdijk: UNESCO World Heritage Windmills**

Kinderdijk is a UNESCO World Heritage site featuring a remarkable collection of nineteen well-preserved windmills, built in the 18th century as part of a water management system. It's a stunning landscape of windmills, canals, and polders, showcasing Dutch water management ingenuity. You can walk, cycle, or take a boat trip through the area.

Practical Tip: Kinderdijk is best explored by walking or cycling. Rent a bike at the visitor center or nearby. Take a boat trip on the canals for different perspectives of the windmills. Visit the windmill museums to learn about their history and function. Kinderdijk is best reached by car or waterbus from Rotterdam or Dordrecht. It's less crowded than Zaanse Schans, offering a more tranquil windmill experience.

- **Volendam and Marken: Traditional Fishing Villages**

Volendam and Marken are charming former fishing villages on the coast of the IJsselmeer lake, known for their traditional Dutch costumes, wooden houses, and harbor atmosphere. Marken is an island (now connected by a causeway) and has preserved its unique character even more strongly. They offer a glimpse into traditional Dutch fishing village life.

Practical Tip: Visit Volendam harbor and see the traditional fishing boats. Take a ferry from Volendam to Marken and explore Marken island. Try fresh seafood in Volendam or Marken. You might see locals in traditional costumes, especially in Volendam, though it's mainly for tourists these days. Volendam and Marken are best reached by bus from Amsterdam Centraal Station (Bus 316).

- **Dutch Coastline: Beaches and Seaside Resorts**

The **Dutch coastline** along the North Sea offers long sandy beaches, dunes, and charming seaside resorts. **Scheveningen** and **Zandvoort** are popular beach resorts with piers, promenades, and beach clubs. The Dutch coast is great for beach walks, cycling along the dunes, water sports (windsurfing, kitesurfing), and enjoying fresh seafood.

Practical Tip: Scheveningen Beach is easily reached by tram from The Hague. Zandvoort Beach is easily reached by train from Haarlem or Amsterdam. Enjoy beach walks, cycling along the dunes, or relax at a beach club. Try fresh seafood at a seaside restaurant. Be prepared for wind, even in summer, on the Dutch coast.

Day Trips and Excursions from Amsterdam

Amsterdam is a perfect base for exploring the surrounding regions and cities on day trips.

- **Zaanse Schans and Volendam/Marken Day Trip**

Combine a visit to **Zaanse Schans** windmills and the traditional fishing villages of **Volendam and Marken** in one day trip. You can take a bus tour from Amsterdam that covers all three, or travel independently by bus to Zaanse Schans and then bus to Volendam and Marken. It's a classic Dutch countryside and heritage day trip.

Practical Tip: Bus tours are a convenient way to visit all three in a day, especially if short on time. If traveling independently, check bus schedules in advance. Start early to make the most of your day. Consider renting bikes in Volendam or Marken to explore the villages at a slower pace.

- **Haarlem and Zandvoort Beach Day Trip**

Combine a visit to the historic city of **Haarlem** with a relaxing afternoon at **Zandvoort Beach**. Take a train to Haarlem, explore the Grote Markt and Frans Hals Museum, then take a short train or bus ride to Zandvoort Beach to enjoy the seaside. It's a great combination of city culture and coastal relaxation.

Practical Tip: Train is the easiest way to travel between Amsterdam, Haarlem, and Zandvoort. Enjoy lunch in Haarlem's Grote Markt square before heading to the beach. Bring swimwear and beach gear if you plan to swim or sunbathe at Zandvoort.

- **Utrecht and De Haar Castle Day Trip**

Combine the medieval charm of **Utrecht** with a visit to the fairytale **De Haar Castle**, the largest castle in the Netherlands. Take a train to Utrecht, explore the city center and Dom Tower, then take a bus or taxi to De Haar Castle (a bit outside Utrecht). It's a day trip combining city culture and castle grandeur.

Practical Tip: Train to Utrecht is easy from Amsterdam. De Haar Castle is a bit less accessible by public transport; check bus connections from Utrecht or consider a taxi or organized tour. Book De Haar Castle tickets online in advance. Allow sufficient time for both Utrecht city center and the castle visit.

- **The Hague and Delft Day Trip**

Combine the political city of **The Hague** with the charming Delftware city of **Delft** in one day trip. Take a train to The Hague, explore the Binnenhof and Mauritshuis, then take a short train to Delft to visit a Delftware factory and explore its historic center. It's a day trip combining politics, art, and traditional crafts.

Practical Tip: Train travel between Amsterdam, The Hague, and Delft is efficient. Start in The Hague and then take a short train to Delft. Visit the Mauritshuis in The Hague early to avoid crowds. In Delft, focus on exploring the Markt square, Nieuwe Kerk, and a Delftware factory.

- **Rotterdam and Kinderdijk Day Trip**

Combine the modern architecture of **Rotterdam** with the historic windmills of **Kinderdijk**. Take a train to Rotterdam, explore the city center and modern landmarks, then take a waterbus or bus to Kinderdijk to see the windmills. It's a day trip contrasting urban modernity with rural heritage.

Practical Tip: Train to Rotterdam is easy from Amsterdam. Waterbus is a scenic and efficient way to reach Kinderdijk from Rotterdam (check waterbus line 202). Alternatively, take a bus from Rotterdam to Kinderdijk. Explore Rotterdam's city center in the morning and then head to Kinderdijk in the afternoon.

Historical Landmarks and Monuments Beyond Amsterdam

The Netherlands is rich in history beyond Amsterdam, with impressive landmarks across the country.

- **Binnenhof (The Hague): Dutch Parliament Buildings**

The **Binnenhof** in The Hague is the complex of buildings housing the **Dutch Parliament**. It's a historic site with roots dating back to the 13th century, located on the Hofvijver lake. You can take guided tours to see the Ridderzaal (Knights' Hall) and learn about Dutch politics and history.

Practical Tip: Take a guided tour of the Binnenhof to see inside the parliament buildings and learn about Dutch democracy. Book tours in advance, especially during peak season. The

Binnenhof is located in the city center of The Hague, easily accessible on foot or by tram.

- **Euromast (Rotterdam): Panoramic City Views**

The **Euromast** in Rotterdam is a 185-meter tall observation tower offering **panoramic views** of Rotterdam's modern skyline, the port, and the surrounding area. It has observation platforms, restaurants, and even "Space Tower" rotating cabins and ziplining for thrill-seekers. It's the best place for a bird's-eye view of Rotterdam.

Practical Tip: Book tickets online to save time. Visit Euromast during the day for city views or at night for illuminated skyline views. Consider dining at the restaurant with rotating views. If you're adventurous, try the "Space Tower" or ziplining. Euromast is located in Rotterdam, reachable by tram or metro.

- **Dom Tower (Utrecht): Tallest Church Tower in the Netherlands**

The **Dom Tower** in Utrecht is the **tallest church tower in the Netherlands**, a landmark dominating Utrecht's skyline. It's a freestanding bell tower, originally part of the Dom Cathedral (part of which collapsed in a storm in the 17th century). You can climb the tower (guided tours only) for fantastic views over Utrecht and the surrounding area.

Practical Tip: Climbing the Dom Tower is a must for Utrecht views, but it's by guided tour only and involves climbing many steps. Book tickets in advance, especially during peak season. Tours start from the Tourist Information Center at Domplein square.

- **Escher in Het Paleis (The Hague): M.C. Escher Museum**

Escher in Het Paleis (Escher in The Palace) in The Hague is a museum dedicated to the works of M.C. Escher, the Dutch graphic artist famous for his mathematically inspired woodcuts, lithographs, and mezzotints, featuring impossible constructions, infinity, and tessellations. The museum is housed in a former royal palace. It's a unique museum for art and math enthusiasts.

Practical Tip: Book tickets online to save time. Escher in Het Paleis is located in The Hague city center, easily walkable from the Binnenhof. Allow 1.5-2 hours to explore the museum and appreciate Escher's intricate art. Check their website (https://www.escherinhetpaleis.nl/en/) for current exhibitions.

- **Mauritshuis (The Hague): Vermeer's "Girl with a Pearl Earring"**

The **Mauritshuis** in The Hague is a world-class art museum housing a small but exquisite collection of Dutch Golden Age paintings, most famously **Vermeer's "Girl with a Pearl Earring"**. It also features works by Rembrandt, Jan Steen, and other Dutch Masters. It's a must-visit for art lovers, especially to see "Girl with a Pearl Earring" in person.

Practical Tip: Book tickets online in advance, especially to see "Girl with a Pearl Earring," as the museum can get very crowded. The Mauritshuis is located in The Hague city center, near the Binnenhof. Allow 1.5-2 hours for a visit.

Arrive early in the morning to avoid the biggest crowds.

- **Peace Palace (The Hague): International Court of Justice**

The **Peace Palace** in The Hague houses the **International Court of Justice** and the **Permanent Court of Arbitration**, key institutions in international law and conflict resolution. It's a beautiful building with a visitor center where you can learn about its history and mission. You can also take guided tours of the palace (limited availability, book well in advance).

Practical Tip: Visit the Peace Palace Visitor Center to learn about its history and international law. Guided tours of the palace interior are limited and need to be booked far in advance via their website (https://www.peacepalace.org/). The

Peace Palace is located in The Hague, a short tram ride from the city center.

- **Cube Houses (Rotterdam): Unique Architectural Marvels**

The **Cube Houses (Kubuswoningen)** in Rotterdam are a set of iconic, cube-shaped houses tilted at a 45-degree angle, designed by architect Piet Blom. They are a striking example of innovative modern architecture and a must-see in Rotterdam. You can visit the **Show Cube Museum (Kijk-Kubus)** to see what the inside of a Cube House looks like.

Practical Tip: Visit the Show Cube Museum (Kijk-Kubus) to see the interior of a Cube House and understand their design. Walk around the Blaak area to admire the Cube Houses from different angles. The Cube Houses are located in

Rotterdam city center, near Blaak train and metro station.

- **Erasmus Bridge (Rotterdam): Iconic Modern Bridge**

The **Erasmus Bridge (Erasmusbrug)** in Rotterdam is an iconic modern bridge spanning the Nieuwe Maas river, nicknamed "The Swan" due to its distinctive pylon shape. It's a symbol of Rotterdam's modern architecture and a striking landmark. Walk or cycle across the bridge for city and river views, especially beautiful at sunset or night when illuminated.

Practical Tip: Walk or cycle across the Erasmus Bridge for city and river views. Take photos of the bridge from different viewpoints along the waterfront. Enjoy the views from restaurants or cafes along the Maas riverbank near the bridge.

- **Delft City Hall: Renaissance Architecture**

Delft City Hall (Stadhuis van Delft) is a beautiful Renaissance-style building located on Delft's Markt square. It's a striking landmark with its ornate facade and tower. It's still in use as the city hall, but you can admire its exterior architecture and learn about its history.

Practical Tip: Admire the exterior architecture of Delft City Hall from Markt square. Explore Markt square and the surrounding historic buildings. Delft City Hall is centrally located in Delft's historic center.

Museums Beyond Amsterdam: Regional Culture and History

Beyond Amsterdam, other Dutch cities offer excellent museums showcasing regional art, history, and culture.

- **Gemeentemuseum Den Haag: Mondrian and Modern Art**

Gemeentemuseum Den Haag (Kunstmuseum Den Haag) in The Hague is renowned for having the world's largest collection of paintings by **Piet Mondrian**, a pioneer of abstract art, including his iconic "Victory Boogie Woogie." It also features a significant collection of modern art, decorative arts, and fashion. It's a must-visit for Mondrian fans and modern art enthusiasts.

Practical Tip: Book tickets online in advance. Gemeentemuseum Den Haag is located in The Hague, a short tram ride from the city center. Allow 2-3 hours for your visit, especially if you want to explore the Mondrian collection in detail. Check their website (https://www.kunstmuseum.nl/en) for current exhibitions.

- **Kunstmuseum Den Haag: Diverse Art Collection**

(Note: "Kunstmuseum Den Haag" and "Gemeentemuseum Den Haag" are often used interchangeably and refer to the same museum.)

As mentioned above, **Kunstmuseum Den Haag** is not just about Mondrian, it has a diverse art collection spanning various periods and styles, including works by Monet, Picasso, and Dutch Masters, as well as decorative arts and fashion. It's a comprehensive art museum with something for everyone.

- **Museum Boijmans Van Beuningen (Rotterdam): Art from Medieval to Modern**

Museum Boijmans Van Beuningen in Rotterdam is a major art museum with a collection spanning from medieval art to contemporary works, including Dutch Masters, Surrealism, and modern design. It's currently undergoing renovation and is partially open at Depot Boijmans Van Beuningen, a publicly accessible art depot where you can see a vast collection of art storage and restoration. (Check their website for reopening updates and details about Depot Boijmans Van Beuningen).

Practical Tip: Check the Museum Boijmans Van Beuningen website (https://www.boijmans.nl/en/) for reopening dates and current exhibitions at Depot Boijmans Van Beuningen. Depot Boijmans Van Beuningen is located in Rotterdam, near Museumpark.

- **Maritime Museum Rotterdam: Port History and Naval Heritage**

The **Maritime Museum Rotterdam** explores Rotterdam's long and important history as a major port city. It features historic ships, maritime artifacts, interactive exhibits, and stories of Rotterdam's port development and naval heritage. It's a fascinating museum for those interested in ships, ports, and maritime history.

Practical Tip: Visit the outdoor harbor area of the Maritime Museum to see historic ships. Explore the interactive exhibits inside the museum. The Maritime

Museum is located in Rotterdam city center, near the Erasmus Bridge.

- **Centraal Museum (Utrecht): Utrecht's History and Art**

Centraal Museum in Utrecht focuses on the history and art of Utrecht and the surrounding region. It features Utrecht paintings, artifacts related to Utrecht's history, and works by Utrecht-born artists like Dick Bruna (creator of Miffy). It's a great museum to understand Utrecht's local identity and culture.

Practical Tip: Visit the Centraal Museum to learn about Utrecht's history and art. See original Dick Bruna drawings and Miffy exhibits. The Centraal Museum is located in Utrecht city center, a short walk from the Dom Tower.

- **Frans Hals Museum (Haarlem): Dutch Golden Age Art**

The **Frans Hals Museum** in Haarlem is dedicated to the works of Frans Hals, a major Dutch Golden Age painter, known for his lively portraits. It houses the world's largest collection of Frans Hals paintings, as well as works by other Haarlem Masters. It's a must-visit for Dutch Golden Age art lovers, especially fans of portraiture.

Practical Tip: Visit the Frans Hals Museum to admire Frans Hals's masterpieces and Dutch Golden Age portraiture. The museum is located in Haarlem city center, near the Grote Markt. Combine your museum visit with exploring Haarlem's historic city center. Check their website (https://www.franshalsmuseum.nl/en/) for opening hours.

- **Delftware Factories (Delft): Traditional Pottery Workshops**

In Delft, you can visit **Delftware factories** to see how traditional Delftware pottery is made and learn about its history. **Royal Delft** and **De Delftse Pauw** are two of the most famous factories that offer tours, demonstrations, and shops where you can buy authentic Delftware. It's a hands-on experience of Dutch craftsmanship and a chance to acquire a classic Dutch souvenir.

Practical Tip: Visit Royal Delft (https://www.royaldelft.com/) or De Delftse Pauw for factory tours and demonstrations. Allow 1-2 hours for a factory visit and tour. You can purchase authentic Delftware at the factory shops.

Delftware factories are located in Delft, easily accessible by tram or bus from Delft city center.

Off the Beaten Paths and Hidden Gems Beyond Amsterdam

For those seeking unique experiences away from the main tourist crowds, the Netherlands offers hidden gems in its regions.

- **National Park De Hoge Veluwe: Nature, Art, and Cycling**

National Park De Hoge Veluwe is one of the largest and most beautiful nature reserves in the Netherlands, located in the province of Gelderland. It features diverse landscapes: forests, heathland, sand dunes, and lakes. The park is famous for the **Kröller-Müller Museum** (mentioned below), located within the park, and for **free white bikes** available for visitors to explore the park's extensive cycling paths. It's a unique combination of nature, art, and outdoor activity.

Practical Tip: Entry tickets are required for National Park De Hoge Veluwe. Free white bikes are available at park entrances – use them to cycle around the park's extensive paths. Visit the Kröller-Müller Museum within the park. The park is best reached by car or bus from nearby towns like Arnhem or Apeldoorn. Allow a full day to explore the park and museum. Check their website (https://www.hogeveluwe.nl/en) for opening hours and ticket information.

- **Kröller-Müller Museum (Otterlo): Van Gogh Collection and Sculpture Garden**

The **Kröller-Müller Museum**, located within National Park De Hoge Veluwe, houses the **second-largest collection of Van Gogh paintings in the world**, as well as works by Monet, Picasso, and Mondrian. It also features a large **sculpture garden**, one of the largest in Europe, with sculptures by Rodin, Henry Moore, and Barbara Hepworth, set in the natural landscape. It's a world-class art museum in a stunning natural setting.

Practical Tip: Book tickets online in advance, especially if visiting on weekends or holidays. The Kröller-Müller Museum is located within National Park De Hoge Veluwe. Combine your museum visit with exploring the national park by bike.

Allow at least 3-4 hours for the museum and sculpture garden.

- **Maastricht Caves: Underground Tunnels and History**

Maastricht Caves near Maastricht in South Limburg are a network of **underground tunnels** created by centuries of marlstone mining. You can take guided tours to explore these caves, learn about their history (including use as WWII shelters), and see cave drawings and formations. It's a unique and adventurous experience, especially on a hot day as the caves are cool.

Practical Tip: Guided tours are essential to visit the Maastricht Caves; book tours in advance, especially during peak season. Wear comfortable shoes and bring a light jacket, as the caves are cool and damp. The caves are located just outside Maastricht city center, reachable by bus or car. Check the website of **ENCI Caves** or **Grotten St. Pietersberg** for tour information.

- **Fortress City of Naarden: Star-Shaped Fortifications**

Naarden is a beautifully preserved **fortress city** near Amsterdam, known for its distinctive **star-shaped fortifications**. You can walk or cycle along the ramparts, explore the historic city center within the walls, and visit the **Dutch Fortress Museum** to learn about its military history. It's a unique example of Dutch military architecture.

Practical Tip: Walk or cycle along the ramparts of Naarden. Visit the Dutch Fortress Museum to learn about its history. Explore the charming city center within the fortress walls. Naarden is easily reached by train from Amsterdam (Naarden-Bussum station) and then a short bus ride or walk to the fortress city.

- **Island of Texel: Wadden Island Nature and Beaches**

Texel is the largest of the **Dutch Wadden Islands**, a chain of islands off the north coast of the Netherlands, part of a UNESCO World Heritage site. Texel is known for its **nature reserves, beaches, dunes, birdlife, and charming villages**. It's a perfect destination for nature lovers, cyclists, and beachgoers seeking a tranquil island escape.

Practical Tip: Take a ferry from Den Helder to Texel (ferry operator **TESO** - https://www.teso.nl/en/). Rent a bike on Texel to explore the island's cycling paths and nature reserves. Visit the Ecomare seal sanctuary. Enjoy birdwatching, beach walks, and fresh seafood. Texel is best explored over a few days to fully appreciate its nature and tranquility.

- **Bourtange Fortress Village: Reconstructed Star Fort**

Bourtange is a unique **fortress village** in the province of Groningen, northeastern Netherlands. It's a fully reconstructed star fort, built in the 16th century, offering a glimpse into military history and life in a fortress village. You can walk around the ramparts, explore the historic buildings, and experience a step back in time.

Practical Tip: Walk around the ramparts and explore the historic buildings within Bourtange. Visit the museum inside the fortress to learn about its history. Bourtange is best reached by car or bus, located in a more remote area of the northeastern Netherlands.

- **Explore Dutch Vineyards: Wine Tasting in the Netherlands**

Believe it or not, the Netherlands has a growing **wine region**! While not as famous as French or Italian wines, Dutch vineyards are producing increasingly good wines, especially white wines and sparkling wines, due to climate change. You can visit **Dutch vineyards** (mostly in the south and east of the country), take vineyard tours, and enjoy **wine tasting**. It's a unique and surprising Dutch experience.

Practical Tip: Dutch vineyards are mostly located in regions like Limburg, Gelderland, and Zeeland. Search online for "Dutch vineyards" or "wijngaarden Nederland" to find vineyards open for tours and tastings. Book vineyard tours and tastings in advance. Combine vineyard visits with exploring the surrounding countryside.

CHAPTER 6

LOCAL CUISINE AND DINING

Local Cuisine and Must-Try Dishes

Dutch food is comforting, often influenced by its maritime history and agricultural landscape. It's about simple, quality ingredients and flavors that warm you up, especially during the cooler months.

- **Stroopwafels: Iconic Dutch Syrup Waffles**

Stroopwafels are perhaps the most iconic Dutch treat. These thin, crispy waffles are sandwiched together with a layer of sweet, gooey caramel syrup. They are best enjoyed warm, often placed over a hot drink so the steam softens the waffle and melts the syrup slightly. The combination of textures and the rich, sweet flavor is simply irresistible.

How to get it: You can find stroopwafels everywhere in the Netherlands – from supermarkets and bakeries to street markets and dedicated stroopwafel stands. For a fresh, warm stroopwafel, look for street vendors, especially at markets like the Albert Cuyp Market in Amsterdam or local weekly markets in other cities. Supermarkets sell pre-packaged stroopwafels which are also tasty and easy to take home as souvenirs.

- **Haring (Raw Herring): A Dutch Delicacy**

Haring, or raw herring, is a true Dutch delicacy, and for the adventurous eater, it's a must-try. Served typically from street stalls or fish shops, 'Hollandse Nieuwe' (Dutch New Herring) is lightly brined and incredibly fresh. It's often eaten by holding the herring by the tail, dipping it in chopped onions, and letting it slide into your mouth. The taste is surprisingly mild and briny, not overly fishy.

How to get it: Haring stalls (often called 'haringhandels') are common in city centers, near markets, and even train stations. Look for signs that say "Hollandse Nieuwe" to ensure you're getting the fresh, seasonal herring. You can also find it in fish shops ('viswinkel'). Ask for 'haring met uitjes' (herring with onions).

- **Bitterballen: Savory Meatballs for Snacking**

Bitterballen are deep-fried, crispy balls filled with a rich, savory meat ragout. They are a quintessential Dutch snack, especially enjoyed with drinks in "brown cafes" or at parties. Served hot with mustard for dipping, the contrast between the crunchy exterior and the creamy, flavorful filling is delightful.

How to get it: Bitterballen are on the menu of almost every "brown cafe" (traditional Dutch pub) and many restaurants. Just ask for "bitterballen" when ordering drinks. Supermarkets also sell frozen bitterballen to try cooking at home.

- **Poffertjes: Mini Dutch Pancakes**

Poffertjes are tiny, fluffy pancakes, cooked in a special pan that creates their characteristic small, round shape. They are light, airy, and slightly sweet, traditionally served warm with butter and powdered sugar. Poffertjes are a popular treat at markets, festivals, and pancake houses ('pannenkoekenhuizen').

How to get it: You'll find poffertjes stands at markets, fairs, and festivals throughout the Netherlands. Many pancake houses also serve poffertjes as a dessert. Look for signs that say "Poffertjes" or follow the delicious smell of cooking batter.

- **Erwtensoep (Split Pea Soup): Hearty Winter Soup**

Erwtensoep, or split pea soup, is a thick, hearty soup, perfect for cold Dutch winters. It's made with split peas, pork (often smoked sausage or bacon), and vegetables like celery and carrots. So thick it's almost a stew, erwtensoep is incredibly warming and flavorful, a true comfort food.

How to get it: Erwtensoep is a winter dish, so you'll find it more readily available in restaurants and cafes during the colder months (October to March). Many traditional Dutch restaurants and "brown cafes" will serve it as a daily special in winter. Supermarkets also sell canned and pre-made erwtensoep.

- **Cheese: Gouda, Edam, and Beyond - Dutch Cheese Varieties**

The Netherlands is famous for its cheese, and Gouda and Edam are just the beginning. Dutch cheese comes in a wide variety of flavors, ages, and textures, from young and creamy to aged and sharp. Beyond Gouda and Edam, explore cheeses like Leidse kaas (cumin cheese), Maasdammer (with large holes and a nutty flavor), and Geitenkaas (goat cheese).

How to get it: Cheese shops ('kaaswinkels') are abundant in Dutch cities and towns. Visit a cheese market in cities like Alkmaar or Gouda (seasonal) for a traditional experience. Supermarkets also have extensive cheese sections. For a tasting experience, many cheese shops offer samples and can guide you through the different types.

- **Frites (Dutch Fries): Served with Various Sauces**

Dutch fries, or 'friet' or 'patat', are thicker-cut fries, known for being crispy on the outside and fluffy on the inside. What makes them truly Dutch is the wide array of sauces they are served with. While mayonnaise is popular, try 'patatje oorlog' (fries with mayonnaise, peanut sauce, and onions) or 'speciaal' (mayonnaise, ketchup, and onions) for a truly Dutch experience.

How to get it: 'Fritkot' or 'snackbar' stands are everywhere in the Netherlands, serving fries and other fried snacks. Just look for signs saying "Friet" or "Patat." Order "friet met mayonaise" for fries with mayonnaise, or try other sauce combinations like 'patatje oorlog' or 'speciaal'.

- **Indonesian Influence: Rijsttafel and Nasi Goreng**

Due to the Netherlands' colonial history with Indonesia, Indonesian cuisine has a strong influence on Dutch food culture. **Rijsttafel** (rice table) is an elaborate feast of many small Indonesian dishes served with rice, offering a fantastic way to sample a variety of flavors. **Nasi**

Goreng (Indonesian fried rice) is also widely popular and readily available.

How to get it: Indonesian restaurants are common in Dutch cities. For Rijsttafel, look for restaurants specifically advertising it, as it's often for larger groups. Nasi Goreng is available in many Indonesian restaurants, "brown cafes," and even some snack bars. You can also find Indonesian takeaway shops ('afhaalrestaurants').

- **Speculaas: Spiced Cookies, Especially During Sinterklaas**

Speculaas are spiced cookies, traditionally enjoyed during the Sinterklaas (Dutch Santa Claus) season in December, but available year-round. They are thin, crispy, and flavored with a blend of spices like cinnamon, cloves, nutmeg, ginger, and cardamom. The warm spices and crunchy texture make them a perfect treat with coffee or tea.

How to get it: Speculaas cookies are widely available in supermarkets and bakeries, especially in the autumn and winter months leading up to Sinterklaas (December 5th). Bakeries often have freshly baked speculaas. Supermarkets sell pre-packaged speculaas cookies year-round.

- **Licorice (Drop): Dutch Love for Licorice**

The Dutch have a serious love affair with licorice, known as 'drop'. Dutch licorice comes in a vast array of flavors and textures, from sweet and salty to hard and soft. 'Zoute drop' (salty licorice) is a particularly Dutch taste that might be an acquired taste for some, but worth trying to experience this unique Dutch candy.

How to get it: Candy shops ('snoepwinkels') and supermarkets have huge selections of 'drop'. Ask for 'drop' if you want licorice in general. If you want to try salty licorice, ask for 'zoute drop'. Start with milder, sweeter varieties if you're unsure about salty licorice.

Dining for Different Travelers

The Netherlands offers dining options for every budget and taste, from quick bites to gourmet experiences.

- **Budget-Friendly Eats: Street Food, Markets, and Affordable Cafes**

Eating out in the Netherlands doesn't have to be expensive. Street food from markets and 'fritkot' stands is a delicious and affordable way to eat. Markets like Albert

Cuyp Market in Amsterdam or Rotterdam Market Hall offer diverse and budget-friendly food stalls. Affordable cafes, especially outside the main tourist areas, often have lunch deals and reasonably priced meals.

Practical Tip: Explore street food markets for affordable lunches and snacks. Look for daily specials ('daghap') in cafes and smaller restaurants, often offering a set meal at a lower price. Supermarkets are great for buying picnic supplies for lunch in a park. Consider eating outside of the very center of tourist hotspots for more affordable prices.

- **Mid-Range Restaurants: Cozy "Brown Cafes" and Bistros**

"Brown cafes" ('bruine kroegen'), traditional Dutch pubs, are excellent mid-range dining options. They offer a cozy, relaxed atmosphere and serve hearty Dutch meals, snacks, and drinks at reasonable prices. Bistros and 'eetcafés' (eating cafes) also provide mid-range options with diverse menus, often featuring Dutch and international dishes.

Practical Tip: "Brown cafes" are perfect for trying traditional Dutch meals like stamppot (mashed potatoes with vegetables and sausage) or uitsmijter (open-faced sandwich with fried eggs). Look for "eetcafé" signs for cafes that focus more on meals. Check menus outside to compare prices before entering.

- **Fine Dining Experiences: Michelin-Starred Restaurants and Gourmet Options**

For a special occasion or a splurge, the Netherlands boasts a thriving fine dining scene, with numerous Michelin-starred restaurants, especially in Amsterdam and Rotterdam. These restaurants offer innovative cuisine, exquisite service, and elegant ambiance, often focusing on modern Dutch or international gastronomy.

Practical Tip: Book Michelin-starred restaurants well in advance, as they are very popular. Explore restaurant review websites and guides like Michelin Guide (https://guide.michelin.com/en/nl/en/restaurants) to find top-rated fine dining options. Look for lunch menus at fine dining restaurants, which can be more affordable than dinner.

- **Vegetarian and Vegan Dining: Growing Options and Recommendations**

Vegetarian and vegan dining is increasingly popular in the Netherlands, especially in larger cities. Amsterdam and Rotterdam have a wide range of vegetarian and vegan restaurants, cafes, and even vegan 'fritkot' stands. Many restaurants now offer vegetarian and vegan options on their menus, making it easier than ever to find plant-based meals.

Practical Tip: Use online restaurant finders like HappyCow (https://www.happycow.net/europe/netherlands/) or VegGuide to find vegetarian and vegan restaurants in Dutch cities. Look for restaurants advertising "vegetarisch" (vegetarian) or "veganistisch" (vegan) options. Ask about vegetarian/vegan options even in restaurants that don't explicitly advertise them, as many are becoming more accommodating.

- **Family-Friendly Restaurants: Places with Kids' Menus and Play Areas**

The Netherlands is a family-friendly country, and many restaurants cater to families with children. Look for restaurants with kids' menus ('kindermenu'), high chairs, and sometimes even small play areas or outdoor spaces where children can play. Pancake houses ('pannenkoekenhuizen') are particularly popular with families and often have play areas.

Practical Tip: Pancake houses are a safe bet for family dining. Look for restaurants near parks or playgrounds, so kids can play before or after the meal. Many restaurants in smaller towns and villages outside city centers are naturally more family-oriented. Check online reviews for family-friendly restaurant recommendations.

Street Food Guide: A Culinary Adventure on the Go

Dutch street food is a delicious and convenient way to experience local flavors while exploring the cities.

- **Best Street Food Markets and Locations**
    - **Albert Cuyp Market (Amsterdam):** Amsterdam's

largest and most famous street market, offering a huge variety of food stalls, from stroopwafels and haring to Indonesian snacks and international cuisine. **Location:** De Pijp district, Amsterdam. **Open:** Monday-Saturday, daytime.

- **Rotterdam Market Hall (Markthal):** An indoor market hall with diverse food stalls, restaurants, and fresh produce. **Location:** City center, Rotterdam. **Open:** Daily, daytime and evening.

- **Weekly Markets:** Most Dutch cities and towns have weekly markets, often on Saturdays or weekdays, offering local produce, cheese, street food, and more. Check local tourist information for market days and locations.

- **Must-Try Street Food Snacks and Meals**

    - **Stroopwafels:** (Already detailed above) Freshly made stroopwafels from market stalls are a must.

    - **Haring:** (Already detailed above) Try haring from a haring stall for an authentic Dutch experience.

    - **Kibbeling:** Deep-fried pieces of battered fish, served with garlic sauce or tartar sauce. A popular seafood snack.

- **Lekkerbekje:** Similar to kibbeling but made with cod, often considered a bit higher quality.

- **Patat/Friet:** (Already detailed above) Dutch fries with various sauces are a street food staple.

- **Oliebollen:** Deep-fried dough balls, dusted with powdered sugar, traditionally eaten during winter and around New Year's Eve, but sometimes available at markets.

- **Broodje haring/ Broodje paling:** Herring or smoked eel sandwiches, for a quick and flavorful lunch.

- **Food Truck Events and Festivals**

Food truck events and festivals are increasingly popular in the Netherlands, especially during the summer months. These events gather food trucks offering diverse cuisines and street food, creating a lively and delicious outdoor dining experience. Check local event listings and tourist websites for food truck festivals happening during your visit.

Practical Tip: Check local event websites or tourist information for food truck festivals and markets happening during your visit. Follow your nose and try snacks that look and smell appealing at markets and street food stalls. Be adventurous and try local specialties you haven't tasted before.

CHAPTER 7

CULTURE, AND ENTERTAINMENT

Local Festivals and Celebrations Throughout the Year

The Dutch love to celebrate, and there are festivals and events happening throughout the year, reflecting Dutch traditions, seasons, and cultural interests.

- **King's Day (Koningsdag - April 27th): National Celebration**

King's Day (Koningsdag) on April 27th (or 26th if the 27th is a Sunday) is the biggest national celebration in the Netherlands. It's the King's birthday, and the entire country turns orange, the national color. Cities are filled with street markets ('vrijmarkt' - free market), music performances, parties, and canal parades in Amsterdam. It's a day of national unity and joyful celebration.

How to experience it: If you are in the Netherlands on April 27th, immerse yourself in the King's Day celebrations. Amsterdam is the epicenter, but celebrations happen across the country. Wear orange clothing. Explore the 'vrijmarkten' for unique finds. Enjoy street food, music, and the festive atmosphere. In Amsterdam, witness the canal parades. Be aware that public transport can be very crowded on King's Day.

- **Tulip Festival (Spring): Flower Parades and Displays**

The **Tulip Festival** in spring (typically April-May) celebrates the iconic Dutch tulips. While Keukenhof Gardens (described in Part 3) is a major highlight, tulip fields bloom across the country, especially in the bulb region between Leiden and Haarlem. Flower parades ('Bloemencorso') are a spectacular sight, with floats elaborately decorated with flowers.

How to experience it: Visit Keukenhof Gardens during tulip season (check opening dates - https://keukenhof.nl/en/). Explore the bulb region by bike to see tulip fields in bloom. Attend a flower parade (Bloemencorso Bollenstreek is a major one - https://www.bloemencorso-bollenstreek.nl/en/). Check local tourist information for tulip field viewing locations and parade schedules.

- **Amsterdam Light Festival (Winter): Canal Illuminations**

The **Amsterdam Light Festival** in winter (typically December-January) transforms Amsterdam's canals and city center into a magical spectacle of light art installations. Artists from around the world create light sculptures and projections that are displayed along the canals, best viewed by boat tour or walking route.

How to experience it: Visit Amsterdam during the Amsterdam Light Festival (check dates - https://amsterdamlightfestival.com/en). Take a canal cruise specifically designed for the festival to see the light installations from the water. Follow the walking route to see installations on land. Dress warmly as it's winter and you'll be outdoors.

- **Sinterklaas (December 5th): Dutch Santa Claus Celebration**

Sinterklaas on December 5th is a traditional Dutch celebration centered around Sinterklaas (Saint Nicholas), a figure similar to Santa Claus, who arrives by boat from Spain and brings gifts to children. It's a festive and family-oriented celebration with parades, songs, and treats like speculaas and chocolate letters.

How to experience it: If you're in the Netherlands in late November or early December, you might witness Sinterklaas parades ('Sinterklaasintocht') as he arrives in different cities. December 5th is the main gift-giving day. Look for speculaas cookies and chocolate letters in shops. Experience the festive atmosphere and decorations in cities.

- **Grachtenfestival (Canal Festival - Summer): Classical Music on Canals**

The **Grachtenfestival (Canal Festival)** in summer (typically August) is a unique classical music festival in Amsterdam. Concerts are held at various locations along the canals, sometimes even on boats or in canal-side houses, creating a magical and atmospheric musical experience.

How to experience it: Check the Grachtenfestival website (https://www.grachtenfestival.nl/en/) for the program and book tickets for concerts. Some free concerts are also available. Enjoy classical music in unique canal-side settings.

- **North Sea Jazz Festival (Summer): International Jazz Event**

The **North Sea Jazz Festival** in Rotterdam (typically July) is one of the world's leading indoor jazz festivals, attracting top international jazz, blues, soul, funk, and world music artists. It's a major event for music lovers, offering a weekend of diverse and high-quality performances.

How to experience it: If you're a jazz fan, attend the North Sea Jazz Festival in Rotterdam (check dates and program - https://www.northseajazz.com/en/).

Book tickets well in advance, as it's a very popular festival. Plan accommodation and transport to Rotterdam for the festival weekend.

- **Oerol Festival (June - Terschelling Island): Theater and Street Art**

Oerol Festival in June takes place on the Wadden Island of Terschelling. It's a unique theater and street art festival that transforms the entire island into a stage. Performances take place in dunes, forests, beaches, and villages, blending art with the natural landscape.

How to experience it: Travel to Terschelling Island in June to experience Oerol Festival (check dates and program - https://oerol.nl/en/). Book ferry tickets and accommodation on Terschelling in advance, as it gets very busy during the festival. Explore the island and discover performances in unexpected locations.

- **Local Festivals Calendar: Monthly and Seasonal Events**

Beyond these major festivals, many smaller local festivals and events happen throughout the year in different Dutch cities and towns. These can include music festivals, food festivals, historical reenactments, local markets, and seasonal celebrations. Check local tourist information websites and event calendars for specific cities or regions you plan to visit to discover local events happening during your trip.

How to experience it: Check local tourist information websites for cities and regions you plan to visit. Search for "events," "festivals," or "agenda" on city or town tourist websites. Inquire at local tourist information centers for recommendations on local events.

- **Traditional Festivals Celebrating Seasons and Local Traditions**

The Netherlands also has traditional festivals rooted in local customs and seasonal cycles. These can include harvest festivals, fishing festivals in coastal towns, regional folklore events, and celebrations of local produce. These festivals offer a glimpse into Dutch traditions and local community life.

How to experience it: Research regional festivals and traditions in areas you plan to visit. Check local tourist information for traditional festival dates and locations. Often, smaller towns and villages are where you'll find more authentic traditional celebrations.

Nightlife and Entertainment

Dutch nightlife is diverse and lively, offering something for everyone, from cozy pubs to trendy clubs.

- **Amsterdam Nightlife: Clubs, Bars, and Live Music Venues**

Amsterdam's nightlife is world-famous and caters to all tastes. From bustling Leidseplein and Rembrandtplein squares filled with bars and clubs to more alternative and underground venues, Amsterdam offers a wide spectrum of nightlife options. Explore clubs for electronic music, bars for craft beers and cocktails, and "brown cafes" for a traditional Dutch pub experience.

How to experience it: Explore Leidseplein and Rembrandtplein for a wide range of bars and clubs. For "brown cafes," wander through Jordaan or city center side streets. Check listings for clubs like Paradiso, Melkweg, and Sugarfactory for music events. Explore the Red Light District area for a more edgy and unique nightlife experience (with awareness and respect).

- **Rotterdam Nightlife: Trendy Bars and Underground Clubs**

Rotterdam's nightlife is known for being trendier and more underground than Amsterdam's. The Witte de Withstraat is a famous street packed with bars, cafes, and art galleries, a hub of Rotterdam's nightlife. You'll find stylish cocktail bars, craft beer pubs, and underground clubs, often with electronic music and alternative vibes.

How to experience it: Explore Witte de Withstraat in Rotterdam for a concentration of bars and cafes. Check out venues like Rotown, Bird, and BAR for live music and club nights. Explore the area around the Oude Haven (Old Harbour) for waterfront bars and restaurants.

- **Brown Cafes: Traditional Dutch Pubs with Cozy Atmosphere**

"Brown cafes" ('bruine kroegen') are traditional Dutch pubs, named for their often dark wood interiors and cozy, intimate atmosphere. They are more than just pubs; they are social hubs, places to relax, chat, read the newspaper, and enjoy drinks and simple meals. They offer a truly Dutch and relaxed pub experience.

How to experience it: Look for signs saying "Bruin Cafe" or "Eetcafé". Step inside and enjoy the cozy atmosphere. Order Dutch beers, 'jenever' (Dutch gin), or coffee. Try traditional snacks like bitterballen or 'kaasstengels' (cheese sticks). Engage in conversation with locals (Dutch are often open to chatting).

- **Wine Bars and Cocktail Lounges**

Beyond beer and "brown cafes," the Netherlands also has a growing scene of wine bars and cocktail lounges, especially in larger cities. These venues offer sophisticated drinks menus, stylish ambiance, and often serve snacks or small plates. They are perfect for a more upscale evening out.

How to experience it: Explore city centers, especially areas known for dining and nightlife, for wine bars and cocktail lounges. Check online reviews and guides for recommendations on trendy or well-regarded wine and cocktail bars in the cities you visit.

- **Casino and Gaming Options**

For those interested in casino entertainment, the Netherlands has casinos in major cities, including Amsterdam, Rotterdam, and The Hague. These casinos offer a range of gaming options, from slot machines to table games like blackjack and roulette. Casinos are typically stylish venues with bars and restaurants.

How to experience it: Look for "Casino" signs in city centers. Holland Casino is the main casino operator in the Netherlands (https://www.hollandcasino.nl/en). Remember to bring valid ID for entry and be aware of responsible gambling practices.

CHAPTER 8

SHOPPING IN THE NETHERLANDS

Shopping Guide: What to Buy and Where

The Netherlands offers a variety of unique items perfect for souvenirs or personal treats. From edible delights to traditional crafts and modern design, here's a guide to what you should look out for and where to find it.

- **Dutch Cheese, Stroopwafels, Licorice, and Food Souvenirs**

The Netherlands is a food lover's paradise, and many Dutch food items make excellent souvenirs. **Dutch cheese**, especially Gouda and Edam, are popular choices. You can find them in various ages and flavors. **Stroopwafels**, those delicious syrup waffles, are another must-buy. Pre-packaged ones are easy to transport, but freshly made ones are a real treat to enjoy while you are there. **Licorice (drop)**, in its many forms (sweet, salty, hard, soft), is a uniquely Dutch candy. Beyond these, consider buying **speculaas cookies**, especially around Sinterklaas time, or **Dutch chocolate**.

Where to get it:

- **Cheese:** Cheese shops ('kaaswinkels') are everywhere. For a wide selection, visit cheese shops in city centers or cheese markets in Alkmaar or Gouda (seasonal). Supermarkets also have good cheese sections.

- **Stroopwafels:** Supermarkets, bakeries, markets, and dedicated stroopwafel stands sell them. For fresh ones, look for market stalls or 'stroopwafelkraam' (stroopwafel stand).

- **Licorice (Drop):** Candy shops ('snoepwinkels') and supermarkets have extensive 'drop' sections.

- **Speculaas:** Supermarkets and bakeries, especially in autumn and winter.

- **Dutch Chocolate:** Supermarkets and chocolate

shops. Look for brands like Verkade or Droste.

- **Delftware Pottery, Clogs, and Traditional Crafts**

For traditional Dutch souvenirs, **Delftware pottery** is iconic. These blue and white ceramics range from decorative plates and tiles to vases and figurines. **Clogs (klompen)**, traditional wooden shoes, are another classic. While not practical for everyday wear for most, miniature clogs or decorated clogs make fun souvenirs. Look also for **hand-painted pottery from Makkum** (Frisian pottery), or **linen and lace from Marken and Volendam**.

Where to get it:

- **Delftware:** Delft itself is the best place, with many Delftware factories and shops. In Amsterdam and other tourist cities, souvenir shops and department stores sell Delftware. For authentic and higher quality pieces, look for shops specializing in Delftware.

- **Clogs (Klompen):** Souvenir shops in tourist areas like Amsterdam, Zaanse Schans, Volendam/Marken. Clog workshops at Zaanse Schans and Volendam/Marken sell handmade clogs.

- **Frisian Pottery (Makkum):** Shops in Friesland region, especially in Makkum. Some specialized craft shops in larger cities might carry it.

- **Marken Lace/Linen:** Shops in Marken and Volendam, some souvenir shops in Amsterdam might have a limited selection.

- **Tulip Bulbs and Flower-Related Souvenirs (Seasonal)**

If you are visiting during tulip season (spring), **tulip bulbs** are a quintessential Dutch souvenir. You can buy pre-packaged bulbs ready to plant at home. Beyond bulbs, consider **flower seeds of other Dutch flowers**, or **flower-themed souvenirs** like prints, scarves, or home décor items featuring tulip designs.

Where to get it:

- **Tulip Bulbs:** Bloemenmarkt (Amsterdam's floating flower market), flower shops throughout the Netherlands, garden centers, and even souvenir shops, especially during tulip season (spring and autumn for planting season).

- **Flower Seeds:** Bloemenmarkt, garden centers, some souvenir shops.

- **Flower-themed souvenirs:** Souvenir shops, gift shops, museum shops (e.g., Van Gogh Museum shop).

- **Dutch Design and Fashion Items**

The Netherlands is known for its minimalist and innovative design. Look for **Dutch design homeware**, like items from brands such as Droog Design or Marcel Wanders, often found in design shops and department stores. **Dutch fashion** is also gaining international recognition. Explore boutiques of Dutch fashion designers in cities like Amsterdam and Arnhem, or look for brands known for their functional and stylish clothing.

Where to get it:

- **Dutch Design Homeware:** Department stores like De Bijenkorf, design shops in Amsterdam's Nine Streets or Rotterdam city center. Concept stores and design boutiques in major cities.

- **Dutch Fashion:** Boutiques in Amsterdam's Nine Streets, P.C. Hooftstraat (luxury), or areas like Arnhem's Modekwartier (Fashion Quarter). Department stores might carry some Dutch fashion brands.

- **Antiques and Vintage Finds**

For unique and one-of-a-kind items, explore the **antique shops and vintage stores** in Dutch cities. Amsterdam's Jordaan and Spiegelkwartier are known for antique shops, offering furniture, art, jewelry, and collectibles. Flea markets, like Waterlooplein Market in Amsterdam, are treasure troves for vintage clothing, retro items, and unexpected finds.

Where to get it:

- **Antique Shops:** Spiegelkwartier and Jordaan in Amsterdam, Denneweg in The Hague, antique shops in cities like Haarlem, Utrecht, and Delft.

- **Vintage Stores:** Jordaan and Nine Streets in Amsterdam, Witte de Withstraat in Rotterdam, smaller vintage shops often found in university towns or trendy neighborhoods.

- **Flea Markets:** Waterlooplein Market (Amsterdam), markets in other cities (check local listings).

- **Art and Prints**

Bring home a piece of Dutch art history or contemporary creativity. **Prints of Dutch Masters' paintings** (Rembrandt, Vermeer, Van Gogh) are readily available in museum shops and souvenir stores. For original art and contemporary prints, explore **art galleries** in Amsterdam's Jordaan, Spiegelkwartier, or gallery districts in other cities. Consider **street art** inspired souvenirs, especially if you've enjoyed street art in cities like Rotterdam.

Where to get it:

- **Prints of Dutch Masters:** Museum shops (Rijksmuseum, Van Gogh Museum, Mauritshuis), souvenir shops, art print shops.

- **Original Art/Contemporary Prints:** Art galleries in Jordaan, Spiegelkwartier (Amsterdam), Witte de Withstraat (Rotterdam), gallery districts in other cities. Art markets and fairs.

- **Street Art Souvenirs:** Shops in areas known for street art (like Rotterdam's city center), some design-focused souvenir shops.

Shopping Districts and Malls

Dutch cities offer diverse shopping areas, each with its own character, from high-street brands to independent boutiques and bustling markets.

- **Amsterdam Shopping Areas: Kalverstraat, Leidsestraat, Nine Streets, Jordaan, Albert Cuyp Market**
  - **Kalverstraat & Leidsestraat:** These are Amsterdam's main **high-street shopping** areas. Kalverstraat is a pedestrianized street packed

with popular chain stores, fashion brands, and department stores. Leidsestraat, connecting Leidseplein, also features a mix of shops, including fashion and shoe stores.

- **Nine Streets (Negen Straatjes):** A charming network of **nine picturesque streets** in the Jordaan district, known for its **boutique shops, vintage stores, designer boutiques, art galleries, and cozy cafes**. It's perfect for unique finds and independent shopping.

- **Jordaan:** Beyond the Nine Streets, the wider Jordaan

area offers a mix of **antique shops, art galleries, independent boutiques, and local markets**. It has a more relaxed and artistic vibe.

- **Albert Cuyp Market:** (Also mentioned in Street Food) A **bustling street market** in the De Pijp district, offering everything from food and clothing to household goods and souvenirs, at **affordable prices**.

- **The Hague Shopping Areas: Passage, Spuistraat, Denneweg**

    - **Passage:** A beautiful **historic covered shopping arcade**, dating back to the 19th century, featuring

upscale boutiques, specialty shops, and cafes. It's an elegant and unique shopping experience.

- **Spuistraat:** A **major shopping street** in the city center, offering a mix of **high-street brands, department stores, and fashion retailers**.

- **Denneweg:** A chic street in the Willemspark neighborhood, known for its **boutique shops, art galleries, antique stores, and stylish cafes and restaurants**. It has a more sophisticated and local feel.

- **Rotterdam Shopping Areas: Lijnbaan, Koopgoot, Markthal**
  - **Lijnbaan:** A **pedestrianized shopping street** in the heart of Rotterdam's modern city center, featuring **major chain stores, fashion brands, and department stores**. It's a central and convenient shopping destination.
  - **Koopgoot (Beurstraverse):** An **architecturally unique sunken shopping street**, located below street level, connecting the Lijnbaan with other shopping areas. It offers a different shopping experience.

- **Markthal (Market Hall):** (Also mentioned in Street Food) An **indoor market hall** with diverse food stalls, but also **shops selling kitchenware, gifts, and food-related items**. It's a culinary and shopping destination in one.

- **Luxury Shopping Streets and Department Stores**

For luxury shopping, **P.C. Hooftstraat in Amsterdam** is the Netherlands' most exclusive shopping street, home to flagship stores of international luxury brands (fashion, jewelry, accessories). **Department stores like De Bijenkorf** (found in major cities) offer a wide range of brands, including high-end fashion, cosmetics, homeware, and more.

Where to go:

- **Luxury Streets:** P.C. Hooftstraat in Amsterdam.

- **Department Stores:** De Bijenkorf (locations in Amsterdam, Rotterdam, The Hague, and other major cities).

- **Shopping Malls and Centers Outside City Centers**

For a more mall-style shopping experience, especially if you are looking for a wider range of everyday items or are staying outside city centers, consider shopping malls and centers located in the outskirts of cities or in suburban areas. These often have a mix of chain stores, supermarkets, and department stores, and are easily accessible by car or public transport.

Examples: Mall of the Netherlands (Leidschendam, near The Hague), **Winkelcentrum Hoog Catharijne** (Utrecht, connected to train station), **Alexandrium Shopping Center** (Rotterdam).

Practical Tip: For city center shopping, explore areas on foot. For malls outside city centers, check public transport connections or parking availability. Nine Streets and Jordaan in Amsterdam are best explored at a leisurely pace, Browse the boutiques. Markets are often busiest on weekends; weekdays can be less crowded.

Local Souvenir Guide: Unique Dutch Keepsakes

Choosing the right souvenir can help you remember your trip to the Netherlands. Here's a curated list of authentic and memorable Dutch keepsakes, and tips on where to find quality items and avoid tourist traps.

- **Curated List of Authentic and Memorable Souvenirs**
    - **Delft Blue Pottery (Authentic):** Look for pieces marked "Delfts Blauw" and made in Delft for genuine Delftware.
    - **Dutch Cheese (Gouda, Edam, etc.):** Vacuum-packed cheese from cheese shops or

reputable markets will last longer.

- **Stroopwafels (Fresh or Quality Packaged):** Fresh from a market stall or good quality packaged stroopwafels are best.

- **Dutch Licorice (Drop Variety Pack):** A selection of different types of 'drop' for a taste adventure.

- **Speculaas Cookies (Traditional Spiced):** Look for traditionally spiced speculaas, especially around Sinterklaas.

- **Jenever (Dutch Gin):** A bottle of Dutch gin ('jenever') is a unique alcoholic souvenir.

- **Dutch Beer (Craft Beer Selection):** A selection of Dutch craft beers, from local breweries.

- **Dutch Chocolate (Quality Brands):** Choose brands like Verkade, Droste, or Tony's Chocolonely.

- **Windmill Souvenirs (Tasteful and Well-made):** If you want a windmill souvenir, choose a well-made, tasteful one, not a cheap plastic version.

- **Tulip-themed items (Scarves, Prints, Home Décor):** Choose items with tasteful tulip designs, not overly kitschy souvenirs.

- **Dutch Design Item (Small Homeware Piece):** A small, well-designed Dutch homeware item can be a stylish reminder of your trip.

- **Antique Tile or Small Delftware Piece (from Antique Shop):** A small antique tile or Delftware piece from a reputable antique shop can be a unique and valuable souvenir.

- **Where to Find Quality Souvenirs and Avoid Tourist Traps**
    - **Specialty Shops:** For Delftware, cheese, antiques, and design items, seek out specialty shops rather than generic souvenir stores.

- **Museum Shops:** Museum shops (Rijksmuseum, Van Gogh Museum, etc.) often have high-quality, art-related souvenirs.

- **Local Markets (for Food and Crafts):** Markets like Albert Cuyp Market and weekly markets can offer good value and local products, but be discerning about quality.

- **Avoid Overly Touristy Areas for Souvenirs:** Shops directly in the most crowded tourist areas (e.g., Dam Square in Amsterdam) often sell lower-quality, mass-produced souvenirs. Venture slightly away from these hotspots for better quality and more unique finds.

- **Look for "Made in Holland" or "Delfts Blauw" Marks:** For Delftware and other crafts, look for markings indicating authenticity or Dutch origin.

- **Ask Locals for Recommendations:** Locals can often point you to good quality shops and markets for souvenirs.

CHAPTER 9

NATURE AND OUTDOOR ADVENTURES

Local Boat Tours and Cruises

Given the Netherlands' intricate network of canals, rivers, and lakes, boat tours and cruises are a fantastic way to explore the country from a different perspective. They offer relaxing sightseeing, access to unique areas, and a chance to appreciate the Dutch landscape and cityscapes from the water.

- **Amsterdam Canal Cruises: Day and Night Options**

Amsterdam canal cruises are almost synonymous with visiting the city. The UNESCO-listed canal ring is best appreciated from the water, offering unique views of the elegant canal houses, bridges, and city life. Day cruises are perfect for sightseeing and learning about the city's history and architecture through guided commentary. **Night cruises** offer a more romantic and atmospheric experience, with canals beautifully illuminated, often including dinner or drinks options.

How to experience it: Canal cruise operators are abundant throughout Amsterdam city center, especially near Centraal Station, Damrak, and Leidseplein. Look for signs advertising "Canal Cruises" or "Rondvaartboten". You can book tours on the spot or online in advance through websites like GetYourGuide (https://www.getyourguide.com/amsterdam-l171/canal-cruise-t11428/) or the official Amsterdam tourist website (https://www.iamsterdam.com/en/see-and-do). Day cruises are widely available, while night cruises often require booking ahead. Consider themed cruises like dinner cruises or wine and cheese cruises for a special experience.

- **Giethoorn Canal Tours: "Whisper Boat" Experiences**

Giethoorn, often called "Venice of the Netherlands," is a car-free village with canals as its main streets. Exploring Giethoorn by boat is essential. **"Whisper boats"** are electric boats that are very quiet, allowing you to glide silently through the canals and enjoy the peaceful atmosphere and natural beauty of the village. You can rent your own whisper boat and explore at your own pace, or join a guided boat tour for commentary on the village's history and surroundings.

How to experience it: Giethoorn is located in the province of Overijssel, about 1.5-2 hours from Amsterdam by train and bus or car. Upon arrival in Giethoorn (usually bus stop or parking area outside the village center), you'll find numerous boat rental companies offering whisper boats. You can rent boats on the spot, especially outside peak season, or book in advance online, particularly for weekends or summer months. Guided boat tours are also available from various operators in Giethoorn. Websites like Giethoorn.com (https://www.giethoorn.com/en/) list boat rental and tour options.

- **Harbor Tours in Rotterdam and Other Port Cities**

Rotterdam, with its massive port, offers impressive **harbor tours** that showcase the scale and activity of one of Europe's largest ports. These tours, often on larger boats, take you through the modern harbor area, past container terminals, shipyards, and sometimes even out to sea, providing insights into maritime industry and Rotterdam's port history. Other port cities like **Amsterdam (port area)** and **IJmuiden** also offer harbor tours, though Rotterdam's is particularly grand.

How to experience it: Harbor tour boats depart from various locations in Rotterdam city center, often near the Erasmus Bridge or Willemsplein. Look for signs advertising "Havenrondvaart" (Harbor Tour). Operators like Spido (https://www.spido.nl/en/) are well-known and offer various harbor tours. Book tickets online or at their ticket offices. Check tour routes and durations to choose one that suits your interests. For Amsterdam harbor tours, look for operators near Centraal Station offering port-focused cruises.

- **Lake and River Cruises in Nature Areas**

Beyond city canals and harbors, the Netherlands has beautiful **lakes and rivers** ideal for scenic cruises in nature areas. Explore the **Frisian Lakes** by boat, cruising through interconnected lakes and charming villages. Take a **river cruise on the Rhine or Maas**, passing through picturesque landscapes, castles, and vineyards (especially in the southern Netherlands). National parks like **De Biesbosch** offer boat tours to discover its unique wetland environment.

How to experience it:

- **Frisian Lakes:** Boat rentals are widely available in Frisian lake towns like Sneek, Leeuwarden, or Heerenveen. Look for "Bootverhuur" (boat rental) signs. Guided boat tours are also offered in many Frisian towns. Tourist information centers in Friesland can provide details and booking options.

- **Rhine/Maas River Cruises:** River cruise companies offer multi-day cruises along the Rhine and Maas, often departing from Dutch cities like Rotterdam or Amsterdam, or nearby German cities. For shorter day cruises, check local tourist information in towns along the rivers (e.g., Maastricht, Nijmegen).

- **De Biesbosch National Park:** Boat tours depart from visitor centers within the park or nearby towns like Dordrecht. Check the National Park De Biesbosch website (https://np-debiesbosch.nl/english-information/) for tour information and booking.

CHAPTER 10

ACCOMMODATIONS IN THE NETHERLANDS

Accommodation Guide by Traveler Type

Different travelers have different needs and preferences when it comes to accommodation. Here's a guide to accommodation types that might suit various traveler profiles.

- **Luxury Hotels and Boutique Stays**

For travelers seeking **luxury and high-end service**, the Netherlands offers a selection of **luxury hotels**, often located in historic buildings or prime city center locations. These hotels feature elegant rooms, fine dining restaurants, spas, and concierge services. **Boutique hotels** provide a more intimate and stylish experience, often with unique design and personalized service. Amsterdam, The Hague, and Rotterdam have a good selection of luxury and boutique hotels.

Examples: Hotel de L'Europe (Amsterdam), The Grand Amsterdam, Hotel Des Indes (The Hague), Mainport Hotel (Rotterdam), The Dylan Amsterdam (boutique). Booking platforms like Booking.com (https://www.booking.com/) or Expedia (https://www.expedia.com/) are good for finding and booking luxury hotels.

- **Mid-Range Hotels and Comfortable Options**

Mid-range hotels offer a balance of comfort, amenities, and price. They are a good option for travelers seeking comfortable and well-located accommodation without luxury price tags. These hotels typically offer private rooms with en-suite bathrooms, breakfast options, and sometimes other amenities like restaurants or fitness centers. You can find mid-range hotels in city centers and suburban areas throughout the Netherlands. **"Brown cafes" and "eetcafés"** sometimes also have rooms to rent, offering a more local and cozy experience.

Examples: Mercure Hotels, Novotel, Bilderberg Hotels (Dutch chain), many independent hotels in city centers. Booking platforms like Booking.com and Hotels.com (https://hotels.com/) are ideal for finding mid-range hotels.

- **Budget Hostels and Guesthouses**

For budget-conscious travelers, **hostels** and **guesthouses** are excellent options. Hostels offer dorm rooms (shared rooms) and sometimes private rooms at lower prices, with communal facilities like kitchens and common rooms, fostering a social atmosphere. **Guesthouses (pensions, B&Bs)** are often smaller, family-run establishments offering simple private rooms, often with breakfast included, providing a more personal touch. Hostels and guesthouses are found in cities and smaller towns.

Examples: Stayokay Hostels (Dutch hostel chain - https://www.stayokay.com/), Generator Hostels, Hans Brinker Hostel (Amsterdam - known for its budget-friendly, party vibe). Hostelworld (https://www.hostelworld.com/) and HostelBookers are good platforms for finding hostels. Booking.com and Airbnb also list guesthouses and B&Bs.

- **Family-Friendly Hotels and Apartments**

For families traveling with children, **family-friendly hotels** offer amenities like family rooms, kids' menus, play areas, and sometimes kids' clubs. **Apartments or vacation rentals** provide more space and flexibility, with kitchens and multiple bedrooms, suitable for longer family stays. Look for family-friendly hotels and apartments in cities and near attractions, or in quieter suburban or countryside locations.

Examples: Many hotel chains (e.g., Novotel, Van der Valk Hotels - Dutch chain) offer family rooms and amenities. Airbnb (https://www.airbnb.com/) and Booking.com are excellent for finding apartments and vacation rentals. Look for "family hotel" or "family apartment" filters on booking websites.

- **Romantic Hotels for Couples and Honeymooners**

For couples and honeymooners, **romantic hotels** offer intimate ambiance, stylish décor, and often special packages or amenities like spa access, canal views, or in-room Jacuzzis. Boutique hotels, canal-side hotels, and countryside hotels can provide romantic settings. Amsterdam, Bruges (Belgium - easily combined with a Dutch trip), and smaller historic towns offer romantic hotel options.

Examples: Canal House (Amsterdam), Hotel Pulitzer Amsterdam, Hotel Dukes' Palace Bruges (Belgium), boutique hotels in Delft or Maastricht. Booking platforms, especially Booking.com, often have "romantic hotel" filters or categories. Look for hotels with "canal view," "spa," or "honeymoon packages" in their descriptions.

- **Business Hotels and Conference Facilities**

For business travelers, **business hotels** offer amenities like business centers, meeting rooms, fast Wi-Fi, convenient locations (often near airports, train stations, or business districts), and sometimes executive lounges. Major cities like Amsterdam, Rotterdam, The Hague, and Eindhoven have business hotels, often part of international hotel chains.

Examples: Hilton, Marriott, NH Hotels, Radisson Blu, many hotels near Schiphol Airport (Amsterdam Airport) or Rotterdam Central Station. Business-focused booking platforms like CWT or hotel websites often cater to business travelers.

- **Unique Stays: Houseboats, Windmills, Farm Stays**

For a memorable and unique experience, consider **houseboats** in Amsterdam or other canal cities, offering a chance to stay directly on the water. **Windmills** converted into accommodations provide a truly Dutch and picturesque stay in the countryside. **Farm stays** offer rural tranquility and a glimpse into Dutch farm life, often in converted farmhouses or barns.

How to book:

- **Houseboats:** Airbnb (https://www.airbnb.com/) and Booking.com have listings for houseboats in Amsterdam and other canal cities. Search for "houseboat Amsterdam" on these platforms.

- **Windmills:** Booking.com, Airbnb, list windmill accommodations. Search for "windmill accommodation Netherlands."

- **Farm Stays:** Websites specializing in farm stays (e.g., search for "boerderij accommodatie Nederland") or regional tourist websites often list farm stay options. Search for "farm stay Netherlands" online.

Accommodation by Price Range

The Netherlands offers accommodation options across various price points, from budget-friendly to luxurious.

- **Luxury (€€€€) Options and Recommendations**

Luxury hotels (€€€€ price range) in the Netherlands typically start from **€250-€400+ per night**. These offer top-tier service, prime locations, elegant rooms, fine dining, spas, and concierge services.

Recommendations: Hotel de L'Europe (Amsterdam), The Grand Amsterdam, Conservatorium Hotel (Amsterdam),

Hotel Des Indes (The Hague), Mainport Hotel (Rotterdam).

- **Mid-Range (€€€) Hotels and Value for Money**

Mid-range hotels (€€€ price range) generally range from **€100-€250 per night**. They provide comfortable rooms, good locations, and often include breakfast and other amenities, offering good value for money.

Recommendations: Mercure Hotels, Novotel, Bilderberg Hotels, many well-rated independent hotels in city centers. Look for hotels with good reviews on Booking.com or Hotels.com in your desired location.

- **Budget (€€) and Backpacker-Friendly Choices**

Budget options (€€ price range) like hostels and budget guesthouses can range from **€25-€75 per night** (for dorm beds in hostels, or basic private rooms in guesthouses). They prioritize affordability and basic amenities, suitable for backpackers and budget travelers.

Recommendations: Stayokay Hostels, Generator Hostels, Hans Brinker Hostel (Amsterdam - if you are looking for a very social and budget-focused hostel), many smaller independent hostels and guesthouses listed on Hostelworld and Booking.com.

- **Free and Low-Cost Accommodation Options (Camping, Hostels)**

Camping can be a very budget-friendly option, especially in summer. Campsites are available throughout the Netherlands, from basic campsites to more equipped holiday parks. **Hostel dorms** are the lowest-cost indoor accommodation. **Couchsurfing** (connecting with locals offering free accommodation) is another free option, but requires advance planning and relies on host availability.

Practical Tip: Camping websites like Eurocampings (https://www.eurocampings.co.uk/netherlands/) list campsites in the Netherlands. Hostelworld and HostelBookers are best for hostels. Couchsurfing (https://www.couchsurfing.com/) requires creating a profile and sending requests to hosts.

Accommodation by Location

Location is key when choosing accommodation. Consider what you want to see and do, and how you want to get around.

- **Amsterdam City Center: Canal Ring, Jordaan, Museumplein**

Staying in **Amsterdam city center** (Canal Ring, Jordaan, Museumplein areas) puts you in the heart of the action, within walking distance of major attractions, museums, canals, and nightlife. It's ideal for first-time visitors wanting to experience the city's core. However, it's also the **most expensive** area for accommodation and can be **crowded and noisy**, especially in peak season.

- **Amsterdam Outskirts: Amsterdam Noord, Amsterdam Zuid**

Amsterdam Noord (North) and **Amsterdam Zuid (South)** are areas slightly outside the city center, but still well-connected by public transport (ferries to Noord, trams/metros to Zuid). Accommodation here is often **more affordable** than in the center and can be **quieter**. Amsterdam Noord has a more alternative and artistic vibe, while Amsterdam Zuid is more residential and upscale in parts.

- **The Hague City Center and Scheveningen Beach**

In **The Hague**, staying in the **city center** puts you close to government buildings, museums (Mauritshuis, Binnenhof), and shopping areas. **Scheveningen Beach**, a seaside resort connected to The Hague by tram, offers beachside hotels and a more relaxed, coastal atmosphere. Choosing between city center and beach depends on your preference for urban sightseeing or beach relaxation.

- **Rotterdam City Center and Waterfront**

Rotterdam city center is modern and architecturally interesting, with shopping, dining, and attractions like the Markthal and Cube Houses. Staying in the **waterfront area** (near the Erasmus Bridge or Wilhelminapier) offers views of the Maas River and modern skyline, and easy access to harbor tours and waterfront restaurants. Rotterdam city center is generally **less expensive** than Amsterdam's for accommodation.

- **Utrecht City Center and Canal District**

Utrecht city center, especially the **canal district**, is charming and historic, with canalside cafes, Dom Tower, and a lively atmosphere. Staying in the center puts you within walking distance of most attractions and restaurants. Utrecht is **smaller and more compact** than Amsterdam, making the center very walkable.

- **Coastal Towns and Seaside Resorts**

For a beach vacation, consider staying in **coastal towns and seaside resorts** along the Dutch coast, like **Scheveningen, Zandvoort, Noordwijk, or Bergen aan Zee**. These offer beach access, seaside hotels, restaurants, and a relaxed coastal atmosphere. They are ideal for summer beach holidays or coastal getaways.

- **Countryside and Rural Accommodations**

For a tranquil escape and to experience rural Netherlands, consider **countryside accommodations** in areas like **Groningen province, Friesland, Gelderland (Veluwe), or North Brabant**. Options include farm stays, guesthouses in villages, or hotels in smaller towns. These are ideal for hiking, cycling, exploring nature, and experiencing a slower pace of life.

CHAPTER 11

PRACTICAL TIPS AND RESOURCES

Travel Scams and How to Avoid Them

While the Netherlands is generally a safe country, like any popular tourist destination, it's not immune to travel scams. Being aware of common scams and taking precautions can help you avoid unpleasant experiences and protect your belongings.

- **Common Travel Scams in the Netherlands and Amsterdam**
    - **Fake Tourist Information/Ticket Sellers:** Individuals posing as tourist information providers

or ticket sellers, often near tourist hotspots, may try to sell overpriced or fake tickets to attractions, tours, or events.

- **"Gold Ring" Scam:** Someone "finds" a gold ring and tries to sell it to you for a low price, claiming they need money quickly. The ring is usually fake and worthless.

- **Pickpockets:** Pickpockets operate in crowded tourist areas, public transport, and markets, targeting wallets, phones, and bags.

- **Taxi Scams:** Unlicensed taxi drivers may overcharge tourists, especially at airports or train stations.

- **"Broken Meter" Taxi Scam:** In taxis, drivers might claim the meter is broken and then demand a higher fixed fare at the end of the ride.

- **ATM Skimming:** Criminals may attach skimming devices to ATMs to steal card information when you use your card.

- **Fake Accommodation/Rental Scams:** Online scams involving fake apartment rentals or accommodations that don't exist or are not as advertised.

- **Tips for Recognizing and Avoiding Scams**

  - **Buy tickets from official sources:** Purchase tickets for attractions, tours, and public transport from official websites, authorized ticket offices, or reliable platforms like GetYourGuide or Tiqets. Be wary of street vendors selling tickets at discounted prices.

  - **Be skeptical of "found" items:** If someone approaches you with a "found" item like a gold ring to sell, politely decline and walk away. It's almost certainly a scam.

- **Use licensed taxis or ride-sharing apps:** Only use official taxi stands or licensed taxi companies. Alternatively, use ride-sharing apps like Uber or Bolt, which provide fare transparency and driver tracking.

- **Check taxi meters:** Ensure the taxi meter is running when you start your ride. If the driver claims it's broken, negotiate a fixed fare beforehand or find another taxi.

- **Be cautious at ATMs:** Use ATMs located inside banks or well-lit, secure locations. Check for any signs of tampering or skimming devices attached to the card slot or keypad. Cover the keypad when entering your PIN.

- **Book accommodations through reputable platforms:** Use established booking websites like Booking.com, Expedia, or Airbnb. Read reviews carefully and be wary of deals that seem too good to be true. Communicate with hosts through official platform channels.

- **Trust your instincts:** If something feels suspicious or too good to be true, it probably is. Politely decline and move away from the situation.

- **Be informed:** Read up on common travel scams in the Netherlands before your trip to be prepared. Websites like the official Amsterdam tourist site or travel advice forums can provide information.

- **Staying Safe from Pickpockets and Petty Theft**

Pickpocketing and petty theft are the most common safety concerns for tourists in the Netherlands, especially in crowded areas.

Safety Tips:

- **Be aware of your surroundings:** Pay attention to your belongings, especially in crowded places like markets, public transport, train stations, and tourist attractions.

- **Keep valuables secure:** Carry wallets, phones, and valuables in front pockets, inside zippered pockets, or in a secure bag worn across your body. Avoid keeping wallets or phones in easily accessible back pockets.

- **Use a secure bag:** Choose bags with zippers and closures that are difficult for pickpockets to open easily. Consider using a crossbody bag or money belt.

- **Don't flash valuables:** Avoid displaying expensive

jewelry, watches, or large amounts of cash in public.

- **Be extra cautious in crowded areas:** Be particularly vigilant in crowded places, on public transport, and when distracted (e.g., looking at maps, taking photos).
- **Separate valuables:** Don't keep all your valuables in one place. Distribute cash, cards, and documents in different secure pockets.
- **Use hotel safes:** Store passports, extra cash, and valuables in a safe in your hotel room when not needed.
- **Make copies of important documents:** Keep copies of

your passport, ID, and travel documents separate from the originals, in case of theft or loss.

- **Report theft:** If you become a victim of theft, report it to the local police immediately to get a police report for insurance purposes.

Made in United States
Troutdale, OR
03/04/2025